WELSH SHIPS AND SAILING MEN

WELSH SHIPS
AND SAILING MEN

J. Geraint Jenkins
translated by Martin Davis, Afiaith

Published with the financial support
of the Welsh Book Council

Cover illustrations:
Main picture – The 63 ton schooner, Eleemusyna,
of Tresaith, Ceredigion, 1852. Built New Quay 1843 for
Thomas Jones of Sarnau. Lost 1863.
Small photographs left to right – Porthmadog c.1905;
Shipyard, Ceredigion, 1870; Llangrannog, Retired Seamen, 1960;
S.S. Sir W.J. Lewis of Cardiff, 1898.

First published in 2006 by
Gwasg Carreg Gwalch, 12 Iard yr Orsaf,
Llanrwst, Wales LL26 0EH
✆ 01492 642031 🖷 01492 641502
✉ books@carreg-gwalch.co.uk   Internet: www.carreg-gwalch.co.uk

Indexed by Mary Meldrum

Contents

PART I – THE SEA AND ITS SHIPS

PART II – THE PORTS OF WALES

Commendation

J. Geraint Jenkins' contribution to our understanding and appreciation of Welsh history is unique. While Curator of the Welsh Folk Museum at St Fagans and of the Welsh Industrial and Maritime Museum he was at the centre of the preservation and interpretation of our national story. He has also published over fifty titles on various aspects of Welsh history. His studies of Welsh rural life include *The Welsh Woollen Industry* (1969) and *Life and Tradition in Rural Wales* (1976). Our knowledge of Welsh fisheries owes an invaluable debt to his study of commercial fishing in Welsh rivers *Nets and Coracle* (1974) and his survey of Welsh coastal fishing The *Inshore Fishermen of Wales* (1991). His *The Ships and Seamen of Southern Ceredigion* (1982) offers a detailed study of one region's rich maritime past while *Ar Lan Hen Afon* (2005) traces the history of the wide variety of industries found on the shores of our major rivers. *Welsh Ships and Sailing Men: The Sailors, Ships and Sea Ports of Wales* is a significant addition to this body of work providing an overview of the development and experiences of Wales' varied maritime communities, placing them firmly within the context of Welsh history in general. In conjunction with his other publications, *Welsh Ships and Sailing Men* also reflects the delicate and intricate relationship between rural, industrial and maritime Wales and confirms the author's position as one of our most prodigious historians.

Robert John Evans, Morol

Introduction

As an official at the National Museum for over thirty years, the happiest period of my entire career was the nine years I spent as Curator of the Welsh Industrial and Maritime Museum. Here in the docks of Cardiff there was a unique community and I took pride in the fact that I was considered to be a member of that community. As the son of a mariner from Llangrannog in Ceredigion, I was by no means unfamiliar with Cardiff, nor indeed with many of the docks from Bristol to Liverpool and from Hull to Glasgow, and one of my happiest childhood memories was accompanying my mother on visits to many different ports. My family have been seafarers since the mid-eighteenth century, and salt water and the high seas have constituted an important part of both my personal interests and academic work.

This book is an attempt to explain the character and qualities of coastal communities and the generations of Welshmen and women who over the centuries have depended on the sea for their livelihood. It is a fairly general treatment of the coastal traditions of Wales, as opposed to a detailed regional study such as those which are to be found, for example, in the works of my old friends, the late Aled Eames and the late Dr Lewis Lloyd. This present volume has relied heavily on the work of both these maritime scholars, together with historians such as my colleague Dr David Jenkins and others too numerous to mention.

I would like to express my sincere thanks to my friend and neighbour, Gerallt Richards, for his painstaking work in preparing the illustrations. It was Gerallt and my late son, Richard, who were responsible for the maps and the diagrams of ships.

Most of the illustrations come from the National

Museum collection, many of them from my own personal collection which I transferred to the archive at the old Industrial and Maritime Museum in Cardiff.

The rest come from sources that are acknowledged individually below each illustration.

J. Geraint Jenkins
Sarnau, Ceredigion

John Geraint Jenkins M.A., D.Sc.Econ.

John Geraint Jenkins is a native of Llangrannog, Ceredigion. He was educated at Penmorfa School, at Cardigan Secondary School and at the universities of Swansea and Aberystwyth. After a period on the staff of Reading University, he returned to Wales as a member of staff at the Welsh Folk Museum at San Ffagan. Following a period as the Curator of the Welsh Industrial and Maritime Museum, he returned to San Ffagan as Director. After retiring to Ceredigion, he undertook various public duties as the High Sheriff of Dyfed (1993) and was a councillor on Ceredigion County Council from 1994 to 2004, acting as Chairperson of the County Council in 2002-3. He is the author of over fifty volumes, in Welsh and English, on aspects of heritage in Britain, and has served as chairman and secretary of a number of national institutions, and as an editor of several publications. He is married to Nansi and has two sons.

PART I – THE SEA AND ITS SHIPS

The Maritime Tradition

The meandering coastline of Wales is almost a thousand miles long. Along it are to be found broad river estuaries, many bays and peninsulas and several islands. Because of its geography, it was almost inevitable that Wales would develop a maritime tradition, which can be traced back to prehistoric times. Fishing off its coasts and along its estuaries and the transportation of people and goods by sea have always been fundamental to the heritage of Wales.

Because sea-based employment was so well established over so many centuries, those communities where seafaring was important quite naturally developed their own character and qualities. Many of the coastal communities, particularly in the west and north, were in fact self-contained, with the sea dominating the lives and consciousness of the inhabitants down the centuries. Coastal towns and villages such as Aberdaron and Nefyn on the Llŷn Peninsula, New Quay, Barmouth and Newport on the shores of Cardigan Bay, and even the capital, Cardiff, owe their existence to maritime trade.

Up until the end of the nineteenth century, when the railway network penetrated even to the most remote corners of Wales, coastal trade was tremendously important to its people. Travelling overland along inferior roads and through passes in the mountains and hills was always an extremely risky business. Exports such as cattle were driven on foot, and wool was carried on horseback, along difficult routes to the markets in England, but nevertheless the transport of merchandise by sea was far more significant. Many essential commodities were delivered to rural Wales through its ports, many of which were little more than open beaches. Much Welsh export was transported in the veritable armada of ships owned by local people who traded the entire length of the Welsh coast. The movement of materials, people and manufactured goods depended primarily on their transportation by sea, and those parts of the coast with sheltered harbours became the most popular locations for the development of settlements. During the era of industrialisation and urban growth, the development of a particular town often depended on its location and the quality of its harbour facilities.

For example, it was because of its sheltered geographical location, which spanned three river estuaries, that the port of Cardiff expanded so phenomenally during the latter half of the nineteenth century. Previously, life in Cardiff had not been inextricably bound to its surrounding hinterland, and then, fortunately, this hinterland became one of the richest iron and coal producing regions in Britain. It is thanks almost exclusively to the harbour facilities that Cardiff grew to become the capital city of Wales; indeed, the sea will once more dominate its future advancement, according to the ambitious plans for its development into the twenty-first century. This city was, more than anything, the creation of Victorian entrepreneurism during an age when the sea lanes were the motorways of the world. Although it had a canal running up to Merthyr Tydfil and a couple of small enclosed docks, Cardiff was basically just a small, insignificant market town up until the mid-nineteenth century. According to one description in 1851, it was a town of some 20,000 inhabitants, and lacked both influence and status. By the end of the nineteenth century it had become one of the most prosperous cities in the country, a centre of trade, and a magnificent port. The development was remarkable in every way. The city's astounding expansion was driven by one powerful objective: the building of a docks complex and the provision of facilities for the global distribution of the manufactured goods of southern Wales. After all, Cardiff was the gateway to the riches of the Vale of Glamorgan, and these valleys may be viewed as constituting the Saudi Arabia of the British Empire during the Victorian and Edwardian Age. As the valleys flourished and the port's resources improved, and as the railways were extended into the hinterland, the fleets of steamships multiplied, and Cardiff became the honey pot to which ship-owners from every part of Europe came swarming for a taste of its ever-increasing commercial success. By 1910, Cardiff was home to the owners of 367 ships that sailed throughout the world.

Smaller towns also owed their growth, if not their very existence, to the quality of their harbours. For example, an old well-established town such as Tenby developed around a Norman fortress, which could be supplied from the sea in time of siege. Despite unabated attacks by Welsh forces on the castle during the twelfth century, the town grew and became an important centre of trade in south-west Wales during the Middle Ages. In 1328, a grant to the town from Edward III facilitated the construction of its first landing stage, and Tenby became an important port for the import of wine from France and the export of locally mined anthracite. The town received its first charter during the fifteenth century and by the Tudor period it was one of the most important ports in Dyfed, actively involved in trade with France, Ireland and ports in the Bristol Channel. The trade was monopolised by a class of municipal freemen – wealthy merchants eager to exploit every available commercial opportunity. Some of them were involved in piracy and in 1563, for example, they provided funding for the ship *Theseus* to make what was ostensibly a fishing expedition to the Grand Banks of Newfoundland. The expedition got no further than the Western Isles of Scotland, where it harassed fishing boats returning from the deep sea fisheries in the northern Atlantic. It was not beneath some of the merchants of Tenby to bribe customs officers to turn a blind eye to the occasional smuggled cargo, nor did they refrain from trading with Spain, the arch-enemy of the Crown at the time.

The majority of the old established ports of Wales are harbours that were developed for military purposes during the Middle Ages, most of the coastal activity of the period being linked to the building and defence of Norman and English castles. The seas around Wales were strategically important and the castles stood in key positions near the sea or near navigable waterways, and were crucial to any attempt by invaders to conquer the indigenous population. There were a few quays where foreign mariners could come ashore and where military supplies could be landed. Most of the fortifications could be supplied from the sea if they were under siege from land, and foreign ships were probably a regular sight in places such as Caernarfon and Conwy, Pembroke and Carmarthen. Very few of these vessels were from Wales and very few of the Welsh undertook long voyages. According to Giraldus Cambrensis in his account of his journey around Wales in the twelfth century, the reason was that there were scarcely any native ships to be found; the medieval Welsh were not very good sailors. To the Normans, the sea was an escape route during their frequent skirmishes with the Welsh princes, and a large number of small ports, which were often built in the shadow of an enormous castle, were of critical strategic importance.

Some of the military ports of the Middle Ages became major commercial harbours later on in more stable times. Towns such as Cardigan, Carmarthen and Caernarfon became extremely active commercial ports in the less turbulent period which followed the Acts of Union. The inhabitants of the coast of Wales began to take more and more interest in the sea and its potential for trade, and in time, an increasing number of ships from Wales joined the fleets from England, France and Ireland that visited the Welsh coast on a regular basis. Early in the seventeenth century, for example, the Pembrokeshire historian George Owen wrote that 'the country especially of late years is fallen much to trade at sea and a great part of the country people are seamen and maryners'. Pembroke was clearly the most important of the Welsh coastal regions: fish, coal, wool and woollen goods were exported from the old ports near the castles of Tenby, Haverfordwest and Pembroke to the rest of Europe and Ireland, and to places along the coast of Britain.

The port of Cardigan owed its existence to its strategic location on the banks of the Afon [River] Teifi. In 1103, Cardigan fell into the hands of the Norman, Roger Montgomery, and he chose a strategic site on the river on which to build his fortress. This location offered the Norman forces a convenient route to the Irish Sea. Inland, the fertile Teifi river valley could be accessed with ease. At a later date, a permanent castle was built half a mile up river from the original site, in an elevated position overlooking a river crossing point. Later on, this broad stretch of water below the bridge would see the development of a large port with worldwide trade connections.

During the Middle Ages there was a great deal of maritime activity on the river, particular in the transportation of wood, and despite the fact that Cardigan Bay was a renowned haunt of pirates, there was substantial trade with Ireland. To the Normans Cardigan was of vital importance, not only because of its strategic location for governing Ceredigion, but also because it was a trading centre through which commercial activities could be controlled and scrutinized. By 1199, when Cardigan received its first charter, it was already a significant port.

During the sixteenth century, Cardigan was doubtless little more than a small, fortified town, handling an equally small amount of river traffic. Following the Acts of Union, which brought political stability to Wales, the coastal trade increased very rapidly. The Navigation Acts were passed in an attempt to increase trade. Piracy, endemic along the coastline of Cardigan Bay, was curbed, and action was taken to promote sea fisheries. The system of revenue collection was reorganised by levying taxes on foreign goods, and coastal activity was given the opportunity to expand considerably. This substantial development ensured that the port of Cardigan would become the most important in the whole of Wales.

During the Tudor period, Cardigan was primarily a herring port, but herring took on such commercial importance that ships from England, Ireland, France and Spain would come to Cardigan to poach the local shoals. Gradually the people of Cardigan began to take a much greater interest in the sea, and by the dawn of the eighteenth century the port had a sizeable merchant fleet. Considerable amounts of salmon, herring, Cilgerran slates, oak bark for the leather industry, beer and wheat were all exported, and a wide range of goods, from Spanish oranges to crockery and cooking utensils, from coal to building materials, were all imported there. By the end of the eighteenth century, the port of Cardigan had reached its zenith and was the distribution centre for an extensive hinterland.

During this upsurge in trade, there was an enormous increase in the demand for ships, and an important shipbuilding industry developed along the north bank of the Afon Teifi below the bridge. Industry was attracted to Cardigan: there was a tinworks at nearby Llechryd and in the town itself a large brickworks was built, whose products were widely exported. In addition to these industries there were those associated with maritime trade. In 1837 there were four blacksmiths working in the town, and the Bridgend and Bailey Foundries primarily produced essential marine equipment for ships. The area around Nant Mwldan was the industrial heartland of Cardigan, and it included a shipyard, a brickyard, a foundry, and a workshop that made pulley blocks for ships. The town was able to sustain three rope makers and three sail makers as well as two anchorsmiths and, in keeping with a busy port, it contained as many as fifty-five pubs.

Further north, herring became something more than a subsistence food and sailors from the coast of Cardigan Bay began to make inroads in a trade which had been the sole province of ships from Ireland. Several sparsely populated coves and open beaches became lively commercial centres for fishing and the export of herring, and gradually small villages grew up on the beaches to support the industry. By the beginning of the nineteenth century, these small coastal villages were centres of a considerable amount of maritime activity, with a very busy import trade but a less substantial export market. Although up until the beginning of the eighteenth century the inhabitants of Cardigan Bay were primarily involved in herring fishing, gradually people came to take an interest in seafaring (and nor was this restricted to inshore waters). Slowly, seafaring became an established occupation and the fisherman-smallholders, similar to those of Brittany, became less commonplace. Some families, who had previously combined farming with fishing on a small scale, now began to specialise in one or the other. Some gave up their fishing activities to concentrate on husbandry; others moved from their farms in the countryside and settled by the sea. The eighteenth century saw the development of a number of coastal communities such as Llangrannog, many of them founded on small inlets that had not been previously inhabited. In many of the coastal settlements of this sort, a shipbuilding industry was established and hundreds of sailing ships were built in these remote villages in the west.

New Quay in Ceredigion became a centre for shipbuilding, although it did not develop until the stone quay was built in 1835 to provide shelter for vessels. New Quay, and nearby Traeth-gwyn and Cei Bach all had shipyards, which not only provided small boats for the flourishing coastal trade, but also large ships intended for deep-sea voyages. The shipyard at Cei Bach was in its heyday during the 1840s, employing as many as three hundred individuals, and it was not unusual to see as many as ten ships on the stocks at the same time.

Along the shores of Cardigan Bay between Milford Haven and Pen Llŷn, it would have been a rare sight to see a dock containing water, and at every port ships had to lie flat on the sand or mud to load or unload. A few harbours, such as Aberaeron and New Quay, would be filled by the tide, and navigable rivers such as the Dyfi and the Teifi had quays all along their banks, but in other ports ships had to be anchored on open beaches. The facilities for handling the cargo at these small ports were primitive and they had to rely primarily on brute force and a bare minimum of equipment.

Of course, on the western seaboard, which did not always produce all essential commodities, a large amount of goods needed to be imported. General merchandise, ranging from crockery to draining tiles, and from iron goods to salt, had to be imported through the small harbours along the coast. By far the most common item to be brought in was fuel, which, in western Wales, took the form of *cwlwm* [culm] – small pieces of anthracite mixed with clay – and fertilisers for the land. The most common fertiliser was lime, made from limestone, which was used to fertilise the acidic soils of the surrounding countryside.

In an area such as the shores of Cardigan Bay, where goods for export were scarce, some ships that visited the isolated coves of Ceredigion would have to sail away with a cargo of ballast. Nevertheless, in addition to the small ports that handled the import of a wide range of merchandise, other harbours were constructed primarily for the export of raw materials that were produced in a particular area. In the north, ports such as Porthmadog, Porth Penrhyn and Y Felinheli almost exclusively handled slates; Aberystwyth concentrated on the export of lead ore; Trefor and Penmaenmawr were harbours for the export of granite, and Amlwch in Anglesey was a harbour primarily used for the export of copper ore from Parys Mountain. In the south, ports such as Barry, which was opened in 1889, dealt almost exclusively with the export of coal, which was also the sole basis for the facilities at Cardiff. Of the record 13.7 million tons of cargo exported from Cardiff in 1913, no less than 10.5 million tons consisted solely of coal.

Iron ore and pit props were imported on a large scale and the port of Cardiff was completely dependent on the heavy mining and manufacturing industries. The dynamic influence of coal is particularly evident in the astounding increase in the ownership of cargo ships in Cardiff. Coal, iron ore and pit props were, of course, directly responsible for steam cargo ships replacing the old sailing vessels.

Just as coal was important in the south, slate was vital in the north-west and, from the late eighteenth century up until the beginning of the First World War, slate quarrying was the main industry of this region. At the height of its development during the mid-nineteenth century, not only were the old established military harbours such as Caernarfon and Conwy used for the export of slate, but a number of new harbours were built to deal with the increased exports. For example, slates from Bethesda were exported through Porth Penrhyn [Abercegin], near Bangor; slates from Llanberis were exported through Port Dinorwig, and slates from Ffestiniog through Porthmadog.

Porth Penrhyn is a good example of a harbour built by a quarry owner specifically for the global export of slate. At the end of the eighteenth century, Lord Penrhyn decided to develop a number of quarries around Llanllechid and in 1790, in order to export the slates, he built a small quay at the mouth of the Afon Cegin. A road was built from the quay to the quarry and in 1801 the great harbour of Porth Penrhyn was built. A narrow-gauge railway was also laid down, and as a result of merging several small quarries into one large one, there was a spectacular increase in production. In 1782, 2,500 tons of slates were produced. In 1819 – 24,418 tons, and in 1829 – 40,200 tons. Penrhyn quarry, which employed some 3,825 men, produced 130,017 tons of slates in 1862. In 1866, as many as 764 ships sailed from Porth Penrhyn to destinations all over the world.

Meanwhile, Porthmadog, constructed by William Maddocks in the early years of the nineteenth century, served several quarries and was the terminal for four narrow-gauge railways – Ffestiniog, the Welsh Highland, Gorseddau and Croesor – and it also saw the development of an important shipbuilding industry.

In the south-west, remote villages such as Abereiddi and Porth-gain were examples of ports that existed to handle the export of a single commodity. Before the nineteenth century, Abereiddi and Porth-gain were two insignificant coves on the northern coast of Pembrokeshire where the occasional cargo of limestone or *cwlwm* would be unloaded.

It was, however, the mineral resources of these two harbours that transformed them during the nineteenth century; both possessed plenty of slate, but Porth-gain also had high quality deposits of granite which had been shattered in some places, leaving a grit that was particularly suitable for the production of bricks.

The 1830s witnessed the earliest attempts to exploit these resources by a number of landowners and local entrepreneurs, but none of them had much success. In 1849, however, the lease was taken over by three businessmen from London and it was their venture which led to Porth-gain acquiring the machinery, kilns and tramways which were required to process this new source of wealth. The slate quarry at Abereiddi was also developed after 1850 and, to begin with, slates were exported in small fishing boats of some 30 tons.

However, because of the open nature of the beach, which takes the full force of the prevailing westerlies, a tramway was built in order to drag the slates along the coast to Porth-gain, where a harbour and several quays were provided for the first time in the 1850s.

From then on, while Abereiddi was still handling the occasional cargo of lime or *cwlwm*, Porth-gain became the focus of most of the maritime activity in this area. Its paving stones were of a high quality and were exported to Dublin, Liverpool and London to be used in the construction of some of the tallest public buildings in these cities. Although the roofing slates and bricks were not of quite such quality as those which could be obtained from other areas, there was, nevertheless, a flourishing trade in these goods to the ports of southern Wales and the Bristol Channel. Late in the nineteenth century, as many as twenty sailing ships could be seen in the harbour at any one time, and by the turn of the century the company from Bristol, which by that time owned the whole concern, had bought six steamers of 350 tons, which were all to be used for the sole purpose of carrying granite from Porth-gain.

By the early years of the twentieth century, the port's trade was given a further boost with a fresh demand for granite chippings to lay on roads. The response to this new demand was the substantial rebuilding of the harbour between 1902 and 1904, and the building of brick hoppers (which still stand today) to store the gravel prior to it being loaded into the holds of the waiting ships. This stone was for use on roads all over Britain and Ireland: in 1909, for example, 3,500 tons of chippings were shipped to Bristol; 4,000 tons were shipped to Newhaven, and several smaller loads went to Bridgewater, Minehead, Barnstaple and London. Small local sailing ships also took cargoes of stone to places in Dyfed: in 1910, Fishguard, Cardigan, Aber-porth, Tre-saith and Aberaeron all received shipments of stone from Porth-gain, usually in association with County Council contracts for repairing roads in those areas.

The main problem with exporting stone from Porth-gain was that the village was not connected to the national railway system, and so the chippings could only be easily transported to coastal locations. After the First World War, Porth-gain began to face fierce competition from similar businesses whose quarries were served by the railways, and who were thus able to transport the products more rapidly and effectively to their destination. By the end of the 1920s, much of the equipment for crushing the rock needed to be replaced and there were problems with silt and sand in the harbour. In 1929 the *United Stone Firm* (which, by that time, was running the show) went into liquidation and the last cargo of granite sailed from Porth-gain in 1931.

A few small loads were transported by road until the 1940s, but these days the stark outline of the stone bunkers and the empty harbour are almost the only reminder to the village of the industry which once operated there.

Some ports in Wales did not depend on the surrounding hinterland for their trade; these had been created specifically as transport terminals for passengers travelling primarily between Britain and Ireland. The short-term ambition of many of these was to develop into major transatlantic ports. The port of Neyland near Milford Haven, for example, was built specifically for the Irish Packet service to Cork and Waterford (a service that owed its existence primarily to the railway), and the neighbouring town, Milford Haven, harboured the ambition of developing into a transatlantic port. This coincided with the construction of Brunel's *Great Eastern*, and visits by that vessel to Milford Haven were commemorated by naming one of its streets 'Great Eastern Street'. In 1866, the *Porthdinllaen Harbour Company* in the north began to develop that port, in the hope that they might supersede Holyhead as the ferry port for Ireland. Further to the south, at Aberdyfi, there were plans to develop the village as the main ferry port between the Midlands and Ireland, and in 1889 *The Western Mail* stated that the new service to Ireland promised to elevate the 'obscure port of Aberdovey to a position of considerable importance'.

The main ferry station for trade between south Wales and Ireland today is Fishguard. One of the problems that weighed most heavily on the British government during the nineteenth century was the question of how to govern Ireland effectively. Effective government required effective communications and, by 1850, there were roads and railways throughout northern Wales linking London to Dublin, but southern Wales did not have any direct links through to Ireland. In the 1840s, Brunel had considered Fishguard as a possible port for a link with Ireland to compete with Holyhead, but these plans were abandoned when the Great Famine began in 1846-7. In 1848, plans were drawn up to run a wide gauge railway to the neighbouring bay of Aber-mawr, and up until 1851 this isolated spot was a hive of activity as workers prepared the way for the arrival of the railway. This plan too was shelved and Brunel finally turned his attention to Neyland, which from 1856 onwards became the packet station for Ireland. For several decades after that, Fishguard and Wdig simply maintained their role as commercial and fishing ports. By the end of the 1890s, however, the railway had reached Wdig under the auspices of the *North Pembrokeshire and Fishguard*

Railway, a small insignificant line which meandered through the Preseli mountains. The attention of the *Great Western Railway* was drawn to the completion of this line, and this company began to take an interest once more in the possibility of using Fishguard Bay as a port for Ireland. Soon afterwards the company bought the line, which was failing financially, and embarked on a very extravagant scheme that involved the laying of ten and a half miles of new track between Clarbeston Road and Treletert, and blasting some two and a half million tons of rock in order to create a site for the harbour station and a new quay in Wdig. The packet service to Rosslare commenced in August 1906 with three steam ships – the *St David*, the *St Patrick* and the *St George* – and in 1908 Irish services were redirected from Neyland to Fishguard.

Having established its service to Ireland, the *GWR* began to consider the possibilities of turning Fishguard into a transatlantic port. Liverpool was the traditional location for the transatlantic flagships of the *Cunard* and *White Star* lines, but both companies realised that they needed a more convenient port for landing London-bound passengers and post. Southampton and Plymouth were already competing with each other for this trade, but Fishguard was the closest port in Britain to New York. In 1909, the pressures exerted by the *GWR* paid off when the *Mauritania* called at the port. The ill-fated *Lusitania* also came to Fishguard, and right up to the day prior to the outbreak of the First World War, the large liners would visit on a regular basis. The dream was short-lived however. Such leviathans were too big to anchor alongside the quay, and they had to be unloaded using a tender. Despite the improvements made to the harbour after 1908, these developments came to a sudden end with the outbreak of war, and these ships were obliged to serve as troop or hospital ships. Apart from the *Scythia*, which called in 1928 with a party of Welsh-Americans on board on their way to the National Eisteddfod in Swansea, the big passenger ships never returned, and Fishguard reclaimed its role as a ferry port for Ireland, a role which it fulfils to this day.

The final category of Welsh ports were the fishing ports. Of these the most important was Milford Haven. Milford Haven became a fishing port almost by accident. The maritime links of the port, which lies on the northern shore of a huge natural inlet, stretch back over many centuries, but the final two decades of the nineteenth century, following the opening of the docks, was the real beginning of its great prosperity. In the years prior to this, there had been many ambitious schemes to develop Milford Haven as a large naval shipyard and as the main transatlantic port, beating both Liverpool and Southampton as the major port for the ocean liners. Early in the first decade of the nineteenth century, the port had been home to a group of seal hunters from Nantucket, but they did not use Milford Haven for very long for this purpose.

The entrepreneurs of the last quarter of the nineteenth century saw the transatlantic passenger market as being the only future for Milford Haven, but following many obstacles to their ambition, the *Dock Company* was forced to recognise with reluctance that the future in fact lay in the development of the fishing trade. 'The Dock Company have not built their great docks to attract fishing smacks,' wrote the correspondent for *The Times* in October 1899, but 'they will not look askance on the great possible development of the fish trade'. In his speech to the half-yearly meeting of the *Milford Docks Company* in July 1890, the Chairman, Thomas Wood, stated:

That much derided and despised fish trade has come in very opportunely for us and yields us a very considerable amount of revenue . . . It is a trade we did not either cater for, or look forward to . . . but it helps to pay, and in fact does pay the expenses of the docks.

Very soon, what had previously been considered as something of a joke industry to be tolerated with reluctance, became the bread and butter industry of the port. In 1889 the ocean-going liner *The City of Rome* anchored at Milford Haven, six miles away from the docks, but after that there was very little transatlantic traffic. Gradually, people came to realise that Milford Haven would have to depend on the reviled fishing industry and relinquish its dreams of becoming a port for ocean liners and 'be content with the more commonplace though no less useful role of a Welsh Grimsby'. Despite this, several vain attempts were made to attain prominence. In 1889, for example, a proposal to run a passenger service every fortnight between Canada and Milford Haven was announced, which would subsequently become a weekly service. The first ship, the *Gaspesia*, arrived in Milford Haven in December 1898; the seventy-four passengers on board (she could carry over six hundred) were despatched on a special train that broke the record for the journey to London, and *The Docks Company* congratulated themselves on their great vision. Neither the *Gaspesia* nor any other transatlantic liner was to visit Milford Haven after that, and during the fifty years that followed, it was the fishing industry which more or less dominated the economy and life of Milford Haven. 'The fish trade is Milford's sole industry,' stated the *Pembrokeshire Herald* on the 30th of August 1912. Everything and everybody in the town depended on it:

Directly or indirectly between 1,500 and 2,000 people are engaged in it. The population of the town has been doubled by means of it and thousands of pounds' worth of house property has been erected as an outcome of its prosperity.

At the close of the twentieth century, the ports of Wales are a mere shadow of their former position and prosperity. Cardiff no longer exports coal, nor does Barry, nor Swansea; Port Talbot is no longer involved in anything but the import of iron ore, and Milford Haven with the import of oil. The slate ports of northern Wales have not seen a cargo ship for many years. The small rural harbours which once provided sustenance for the local inhabitants are no more than tourist attractions. Holyhead, Fishguard and Pembroke Dock are still active as ferry stations to Ireland, but in Wales, generally speaking, the maritime tradition has died.

Shipbuilders

The last quarter of the eighteenth century saw a development in the shipbuilding industry, in the face of a big demand for vessels for the export and import of goods. The construction of ships, both large and small, became one of the main activities along the Welsh seaboard. This expertise developed not only in the coastal villages but also in places that were fairly remote and at quite a distance from the sea. For example, in order to export salt herring from the beach at Penbryn in Ceredigion, a number of local fishermen decided to build a single-masted 24-ton vessel at a location some half a mile from the sea. In 1777 the *Blessing* was launched after having been dragged and rolled through Cwm Lladron to the water's edge and began many years of trading across the Irish Sea.

To build a wooden ship required little more than a flat piece of land, if possible close to the sea or a river, with a saw-pit to prepare timber, and the means to bend it into shape. Numerous rural carpenters became highly skilled and confident in this work, with many of them also working as wheelwrights.

Some villages not only built one or two ships but became renowned as major construction centres. In south Ceredigion, apart from the occasional ship built at places such as Penbryn, Tre-saith, Cwmtydu and Hen Fynyw, the industry developed in a number of specific settlements. In the New Quay area, where almost three hundred ships were built, large and small, the industry was so important that the authorities identified three separate locations – New Quay itself, Traeth-gwyn (nowadays the site of a huge caravan park) and Cei Bach (or 'Q bach' as it was called in Lloyd's Register). To the south of New Quay, a number of comparatively small ships were built on the banks of the Afon Teifi in Cardigan itself, and in Llandudoch, while there were particularly active locations at Newport and Fishguard in north Pembrokeshire, where a number of relatively large vessels were built. Aberystwyth was an important centre for shipbuilding, and to the north several ships were built on the Afon Dyfi at Derwen-las, and the Afon Wnion at Llanelltyd near Dolgellau, a fair distance from Barmouth, which itself was an early shipbuilding centre. Beyond doubt, the most important of the shipbuilding centres in western and northern Wales were Porthmadog and Pwllheli. Such was the extent of the industry at Pwllheli that it was described as 'The Welsh Emporium for Shipbuilding'. If Pwllheli was a shipbuilding supermarket, Porthmadog was the boutique, which supplanted Pwllheli in the final decade of the nineteenth century. The workmanship of Porthmadog ships was so superlative that those which were laid down between 1891 and 1913 – particularly the schooners – were referred to as *Western Ocean Yachts*. These ships were considered comparable to the *Fleetwing* and the *Dorothy*, the *M.A. James* and the *Pride of Wales*, as examples of perfection in craftsmanship and design. Of course, these craftsmen were building graceful wooden sailing ships at a time when such ships had begun to be replaced on the ocean by iron ships driven by steam. In the face of competition, the perfection and artistry of an ancient craft were being extolled in the days of its demise.

Types of Ship

The wooden ships built in Wales varied quite considerably from port to port and the owner of a ship would often have an influence on the design of a particular vessel. Nevertheless, ships could be categorised into several universal types.

A. SMACK or SLOOP: A small single-masted ship which was generally used for coastal voyages. Very often a crew of three – the captain and his mate and a young lad – would be sufficient for a smack. Many of the skippers who would become great sea captains later on in their careers started out in smacks or sloops. Although most Welsh sloops were coastal vessels, it was quite common for some to sail to the European continent during the summer months. Flat-bottomed, in order to lie on the beaches, and with a single mast carrying a fore-and-aft sail, smacks could be difficult to handle, particularly in rough weather. Each of these craft weighed less than 73 tons.

B. KETCH: A two-masted ship, the foremast being longer than the mizzen with fore-and-aft sails. Although a number of these vessels, which were also known as *dandies*, were sailing the Welsh coasts during the last quarter of the nineteenth century, very few were built in Wales. For example, of the seventeen ketches sailing from ports in south Ceredigion in 1895, only seven of them had been built in the area and most of these had been adapted from sloops by adding a mizzen mast.

C. BRIG: A two-masted, square-rigged ship. In Wales the brig was the most common ocean sailing – as opposed to coastal – vessel. During the nineteenth century, a large number of Welsh brigs were part of the Newfoundland fishing trade, whereby fish from the fisheries of the Grand Banks were exported to Italy and other Mediterranean countries. These ships, with a crew of some eight or nine, would cross the Atlantic or sail to Britain from Mediterranean ports with wine, fruit and olive oil. Often, a resident artist in a port such as Naples would paint a picture of the ship to sell to the captain. These can still be seen adorning the walls of homes on the coast.

Another form of the brig was the 'brigantine' – a ship with a square-rigged foremast and fore-and-aft sails on the mizzen mast.

D. SCHOONER: Two-masted ships with sails fore-and-aft. There were also three-masted schooners. The schooner was probably the most common of all the Welsh sailing ships. It was considered to be a much easier craft to handle than the brig and the other square-riggers. The schooner did not require as big a crew. In the history of shipbuilding in Wales, the schooner was the most common type. Between 1810 and 1878, for instance, seventy-nine schooners were built at New Quay compared with thirteen brigs, ten brigantines and three barques. Some fifteen schooners between 75 and 100 tons were built at Pwllheli and about nine at Nefyn.

E. BARQUE: A three-masted ship, square-rigged on the fore- and mainmast and fore-and-aft sails on the mizzen mast. A considerable number of these were built in ports such as Porthmadog in the final decade of the nineteenth century. They were extremely important in the slate trade, shipping slate from the ports of northern Wales to all parts of the world. They were also popular in the copper trade from Swansea to south America and in the turbulent nitrate and *guano* trade from Chile and Peru to Europe. Many of the barques owned by the Welsh had been bought in Quebec and Prince Edward Island in Canada. Although some of the ships for the copper trade had been built on the banks of the Afon Nedd [River Neath], most of the vessels from Swansea were from Prince Edward Island. They carried dangerous cargoes of copper ore and coal. Their

The S.S. Sea Flower, *of Cardigan* (Aberteifi) *built in Glasgow in 1876 a regular trader between London and Bristol and West Wales. (D.V.T. Davies)*

The Olwen *unloading a cargo of timber at the Mercantile wharf Cardigan. c.1890.*

The fishing boat **Kirkland** *and a fleet of Milford Haven*
(Aberdaugleddau) *fishing boats arriving in the harbour.*

One of the 'Aberystwyth Ships' – the College Line *–* Breconian
owned by the John Mathias Company of Aberystwyth and Cardiff.

The S.S. Gwenllian Thomas, *the first ship owned by the famous company Evan Thomas Radcliffe from Cardiff, 1882.*

The S.S. Italiana, *a vessel belonging to the Jenkins Bros., whose roots were in Aber-porth in Ceredigion. The* Italiana *was built in Glasgow, 1898.*

Captain Daniel Jenkins of Tre-saith and the crew of the
S.S. Italiana *in Antwerp, 1905.*

The S.S. Aberporth, *built on the banks of the Tyne, 1886. It was*
bought by Daniel Jenkins of Aber-porth in 1903 but foundered in
1904.

The Glanavon *of Nefyn – a barque, built by J.B. Jarrett in 1862 (S. Campbell Jones,* Welsh Sail *1979).*

The Fleetwing *of Porthmadog, built by Richard Jones, Borth-y-gest, 1876. (Gwynedd Archives)*

The S.S. Pontwen, *a ship belonging to the W.C. and C.T. Jones Company, Cardiff, in 1914.*

The S.S. Teifi *near Llandudoch around 1936. This belonged to a local company 'The British Isles Coasters Limited'. (D.V.T. Davies)*

FOR BRISTOL, DIRECT,

Now Loading at Cardigan Quay, and will sail immediately.

A CONSTANT TRADER,

THE NEW FAST-SAILING SMACK,

MARY, A. 1.

John Griffiths, Commander,

(Late of the Trader, Expedition.)

N. B. The above named Commander hereby engages to keep his said Smack, Mary, as a regular Trader between Bristol and Cardigan henceforth, and not to remain a longer period than 10 Days Loading at Bristol at any one time (that is to say) to clear out on the 18th Day after his entry outwards at the Customhouse there, with or without a full and complete Cargo (Reserving to himself the power of clearing out on any Day, previous to the 18th Day, if a full and Complete Cargo be on board the said Vessel) or forfeit the Sum of TWENTY POUNDS to any Shipper or Shippers on the said Vessel from time to time. Due notice will be given by the Cardigan Crier of the Day of the said Trader's entry outwards at the Customhouse Bristol, to enable parties to know the certain day of departure from there.

Cardigan, 24 May, 1827.

[Printed by J. Thomas, Cardigan

Two smacks waiting for the tide near Traeth y Llongau,
Aber-porth.

New Quay (Ceinewydd) – *the most important of Ceredigion's shipbuilding centres.*

The Nymph, *a barquentine, built by Evan Daniel, Cei Bach, 1872.*

The Welsh Back *in Bristol circa 1880.*

S.S. Wimborne – *a Cardiff tramp steamer built at Stockton on Tees for Evan Thomas Radcliffe in 1911.*

Re-union of Master Mariners at Aberystwyth Castle, 1938.

Coastguards at Gwbert, Cardigan, 1901.

The end of the Gracie *near Cadiz, Spain, 1912
(Gwynedd Archive).*

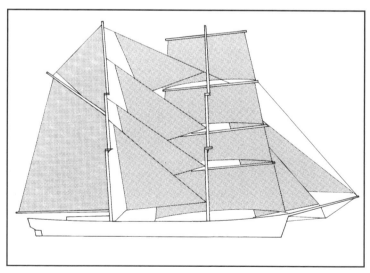

Brigantine

Irish Ferry at Neyland

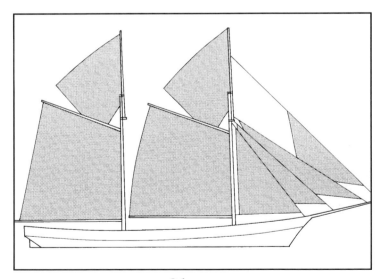

Schooner

The three-masted schooner Gracie *of Porthmadog.*

Captain O.H. Owen and the crew of the Gracie, *May 1913.*
(Gwynedd Archives).

The fine fast-sailing first class Ship,

TRITON,

Of Cardigan, (David Rees, Master,) burthen 400 Tons, will be fitted out for Emigrants, with every necessary accommodations, and will sail on or about the latter end of February, 1841,

FROM

CARDIGAN FOR NEW YORK,

UNITED STATES OF AMERICA.

The second Marquis of Bute (1793-1848). One of the main developers of Cardiff docks.

NOW LOADING,

AT

Pickle-herring Wharf,

SOUTHWARK, LONDON,

FOR CARDIGAN,

'E FAST-SAILING

Smack Ecton,

EVAN REES, MASTER.

Persons des'rous of availing themselves of this opportunity will apply to the Captain on board, or to Mr. D. Davies, Merchant, Cardigan.

One of Swansea's copper ships in dry dock (Swansea Museum).

The schooner Tirsah *from Aberystwyth.*

The S.S. W.T. Lewis, *one of Cardiff's tramp steamers, 1898.*

Coastal ships waiting to be loaded in Cardiff circa 1880.

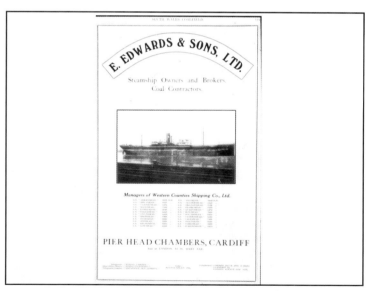

An advertisement for the Edgar Edwards Company circa 1920.

David Williams' yard, Porthmadog around 1900. The ship could be the Isallt *or the* R.J. Owens *(Gwynedd Archives).*

Pegging planks in the ship's frame.

*The workers in David Williams' yard. The ship could be
the* Isallt *or the* R.J. Owens.

*Shipbuilding on the banks of the Teifi in Cardigan circa 1870.
(D.V.T. Davies)*

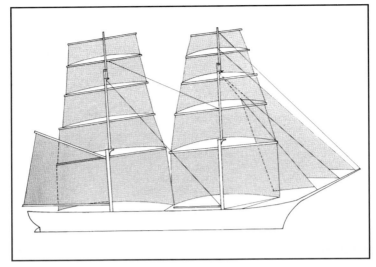

Brig

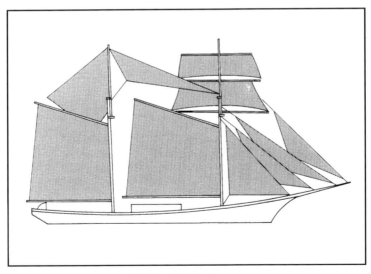

A 'Top-Sail' schooner

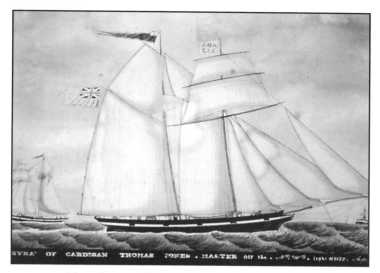

The schooner Eleemosyna, *1852, of Tre-saith.*

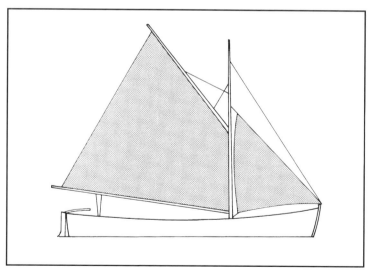

A flat

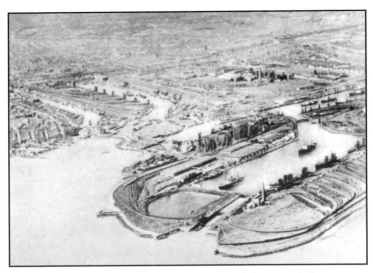

A view of Cardiff docks at the beginning of the twentieth century.

The Margaret Ann *(the crockery ship) and the* Eliza Jane
on Llangrannog beach circa 1895.

Aberystwyth harbour circa 1880.

Cardiff shipowners at their headquarters: the Coal Exchange in Mount Stuart Square, 1916.

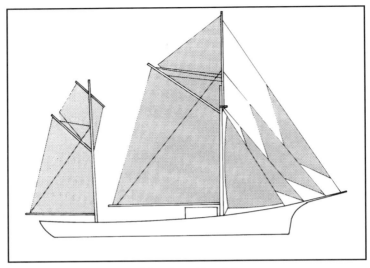

A ketch or 'dandy'.

The schooner **Robert Morris** *of Porthmadog, built in 1876
(Gwynedd Archives).*

owners were described as being very mean and merciless, and it is hardly surprising that as many as two hundred ships from Swansea were lost between 1873 and 1899. Where speed was not important, the big sailing ships remained popular at Swansea until 1914.

F. BARQUENTINE: A version of the barque that was considered to be easier to handle. The foremast was square-rigged, with fore-and-aft sails on the mainmast and the mizzen. A few of these were built at a time when the age of sail was drawing to a close, most of them at Porthmadog and Borth-y-gest.

G. SNOW: A two-masted ship, square-rigged on both masts in the same way as a barque, carrying a third fore-and-aft sail on a smaller after mast. These were popular at the beginning of the nineteenth century in Ceredigion and renowned ships such as the *Triton*, the *Active* and the *Albion* were reputedly vessels of this type, vessels that played a vital role in emigration from Wales to the United States during the first half of the nineteenth century. A number of these ships were built in Newport, Pembrokeshire, by a notable shipbuilding family, the Harvards.

H. FLAT: This was a type of sloop immortalised in the Welsh folk song 'Fflat Huw Puw'. There were no guardrails on the decks of these vessels. Originally from the River Mersey, they were used regularly along the northern coast of Wales. Another version of the flat was the Severn Trow, which operated in the western reaches of the Severn Estuary on the Afon Gwy [River Usk] from Chepstow as far as Hereford.

In the final years of the nineteenth century, Captain Thomas Picton Richards, shipowner and agent for his brother, William Richards – who had married the daughter of James Yeo, a shipbuilder from Prince Edward Island – sold cheap ships in Wales. To a great extent, it was these two, the Richards Brothers, who contributed to the demise of shipbuilding in Wales, as their product was much cheaper than the home-built ships.

Apart from shipbuilders, there were other craftsmen who were of vital importance to shipbuilding. In the days of sailing ships, almost every port had its complement of sail and rope makers, pulley block makers and blacksmiths. In 1859 in the town of Cardigan, for example, there were seven shipyards, two blacksmiths who specialised in the forging of anchors and chains, three pulley block makers, three rope makers and three sail makers. Two foundries grew up in the town – the Bridgend Foundry and Bailey's Foundry, and both were essential to the shipping industry.

At Pwllheli in 1841, to give a further example, there were five shipbuilders, thirty-five carpenters involved with the maritime industry, nine sawyers, one pulley block maker, seven painters and seven smiths.

Building Methods

The construction of ships, naturally enough, required timber – oak in particular. In many places, timber from the area around the port was used. The ships at Llangrannog, for example, used oak from the Bronwydd estate near Henllan some ten miles away. Before very long, it was discovered that there was insufficient timber locally to meet the demand, and very soon an import trade had developed to bring timber from Scandinavia and the Baltic.

In shipbuilding along the coast of Wales, the usual practice was for the builder to make a model of the proposed vessel. The model would then be shown to the customer and modified according to the customer's requirements. The lines of the wooden model would be transferred to the workshop floor and the timber cut to size and steamed to construct the ship's hull. To make it watertight required the preparation of oakum – old rope mixed with pitch and pressed in between the planks and deckings of the ships. Since a large number of Welsh ships would be operating in rough seas, the caulking of vessels was a regular task.

Investing in ships

In the early days of sailing ships from the latter part of the eighteenth century to the mid-nineteenth century, the finance for building a ship was raised locally. Apart from the ship's master, who usually owned a number of shares – sometimes just a single share out of sixty-four – there would also be the craftsmen responsible for its construction – the carpenters and blacksmiths, the rope and sail makers – who would also hold several shares. For those individuals to whom the ship was most useful (farmers and the owners of quarries and coalmines, merchants and industrialists) a share in a ship was considered essential. Then there were those who had nothing to do with trading, but who simply invested in ships. Among these were the occasional squire and clergyman, schoolmaster and widow who dreamed of fortune and substantial profits in the years to come. Far too often their confidence was misplaced, as losses among sailing ships were a frequent occurrence.

In time, traders who were responsible for the

distribution of goods from the ports became much more important in ship ownership than the small-scale investor. By 1826, for example, seven traders from Cardigan owned ships and held the majority of shares in all of them: individuals such as William Phillips, owner of the *Waterloo* and the *William and Nelly*, for example, or the Stephens family from Llechryd and the Lloyds from Coedmor, who ran five ships used exclusively for the export of Cilgerran slate from Cardigan.

The sailing ship was the main means of trading and transport for many of the shoreline communities and it was useful for members of the community to be able to state their interest in a ship through investment. For example, the Register of the schooner *Nina*, built on the shores of the Afon Teifi in 1825, shows this 97-ton vessel as having several owners:

John Griffiths, Master	8 shares
Thomas Griffiths, Gentleman	4 shares
John Evans, Merchant	4 shares
Thomas Wright, Esquire	4 shares
Daniel Davies, Mariner	2 shares
David Davies, Culm Merchant	2 shares
Thomas Thomas, Victualler	2 shares
Morgan Jenkins, Mercer	2 shares
Evan Davis (Treforgan) Esquire	2 shares
David Richards, Farmer	12 shares
Thomas George, Farmer	4 shares
David Griffiths, Farmer	4 shares
Jane Evans, Farmer	2 shares
David Morris, Farmer	2 shares
Thomas Richards, Farmer	2 shares
John Owen, Farmer	2 shares
John Edwards, Merchant	4 shares
Thomas Thomas, Farmer	2 shares

The cost of building a sailing ship could vary enormously from area to area, depending mainly on the size of the vessel involved. For example, the sloop *Catherine* from New Quay cost £822 12s. in 1825, and the brigantine *Nymph* from the same port £2,450 in 1872. John Parry, of Y Ship, Tre-saith, paid £920 to John Williams, the shipbuilder from Cardigan, for the sloop *Margaret Anne* in 1875. Very often, payment for construction had to be made while the work was still in progress – as, for example, in this 1833 reference to Thomas Davies, one of the builders from Traeth-gwyn near New Quay, who asked for:

> Thirty two pounds when the foot and stem and floorings laid in; forty pounds when frames and Keelson laid in, fifty six pounds when the hull is completed ready for launch.

Thomas Davies and his son John were the most important among the shipbuilders of Traeth-gwyn, and apart from the sloop *Nel* mentioned above, during the ensuing years they were to build the *Hope*, the *Osprey*, the *Maria*, the *Anne and Mary*, the *Affines*, the *Hedesia*, the *Hawendale*, the *Rosina*, the *U. Larsing* (named after someone from India who had come under the influence of missionaries from Wales), the *Ceredig* and the *Dreadnought*. Between 1833 and 1866, Thomas Davies' shipyard was responsible for building schooners, a brig and a brigantine, mainly for the shipowners of New Quay and Llangrannog.

The shipwrights of the Welsh coast certainly demonstrated first-rate craftsmanship, and the majority of the ships that came from Welsh shipyards were able to sail to all parts of the world and were sufficiently sturdy to withstand the gales that rage along the open and rugged coastline of Wales. Despite this widespread success throughout Wales, the transition to the building of iron and steel ships powered by steam engines never occurred. During the second half of the nineteenth century, steam was rapidly replacing sail throughout the world but strangely enough Wales failed to exploit this enormous trading opportunity. The makers of the *Western Ocean Yachts* of Porthmadog were still producing their magnificent sailing ships up until 1913, and the shipowners of Swansea, renowned for their cautious, parsimonious nature, still used vessels of inferior quality from north America up until the beginning of the war in 1914.

Yet it could be assumed that Wales, in particular southern Wales, had all the necessary resources to develop centres for the building of steamships – resources that were as favourable as those enjoyed at ports on the rivers Tyne, Tees and Clyde. There were furnaces and plenty of coal to produce iron and steel, and there was a good depth in the rivers for launching large ships. A number of steamers were built along the banks of the Afon Gwy in Chepstow, together with a few in Swansea and Neath, and, despite its distance from the iron and steel works and coalfield, a number of warships and *Royal Yachts* were built on the shore of the Afon Cleddau at Pembroke Dock. In Anglesey, William Thomas of Amlwch soon realised the advantage of moving to the port of Millom in north-west England within reach of the Cumbrian coalfield and furnaces.

An attempt was made to develop a shipbuilding industry on the Afon Taf at Cardiff, and *The Western Mail* was full of confidence that Tiger Bay would become just as important as Glasgow. In November 1864, the 700-ton paddle steamer *Mallorca* was launched, and *The Western Mail* published a picture of the V.I.P.s of Cardiff holding up an iron plate bearing the inscription: 'Cardiff Steel for Cardiff Ships'.

Their ambition was to be thwarted, however, and the banks of the Afon Taf were never developed like those of the Tyne and Wear, Tees and Clyde.

Only one company ventured into the field of shipbuilding: *Morel Brothers*, a company from Jersey, whose roots lay in the potato trade with Wales. In 1837, Philip Morel established himself in Cardiff and in 1862 he was followed by his brother Thomas. The language the company used was French and its offices were in Stuart Street in the docks at Cardiff. As a shipping company it was extremely successful, in particular in trade to south America. They were one of the few shipping companies that saw any future in shipbuilding on the banks of the Afon Taf. A site was purchased which later became known as the *Bute Shipbuilding Engineering and Dry Dock Co.* near the Clarence Bridge. Only three ships were built there, as a consequence of legal difficulties with the Bute Estate concerning the purchase of land, and the unwillingness of other firms in Cardiff to support another company. They preferred to look towards England and Scotland than to give any consideration to another local shipping company. Strangely enough, the *S.S. Collivaud*, which was built on the Afon Taf in 1887, sailed for almost three quarters of a century under a Turkish flag. She was broken up in 1958.

Despite the large demand for ships to carry Welsh industrial goods all over the world, and the astounding development of the coal industry in particular, almost every ship in southern Wales was a foreign vessel.

For example, the Morels' company had twenty-five steamships in 1888. They were built by:

E.S. Swan & Co., Newcastle – (1 ship)
Palmer's Shipbuilding & Iron Co. Ltd., Jarrow on
      Tyne (15 ships)
Richardson Duck & Co., Stockton on Tees (1 ship)
William Doxford, Sunderland (2 ships)
J. Redhead and Company, South Shields (1 ship)
Wm Pickersgill & Sons, Sunderland (4 ships)
Kish Boolds & Co., Sunderland (1 ship)
Oswald Mordaunt, Southampton (1 ship)
Blyth Shipbuilding Co., Blyth (1 ship)

When Frederick Jones from Cardiff established his
Abbey Line of comparatively small ships in 1901, which
came to an end in 1960, the ships without exception
came from north-east England, from firms such as
Thomas Turnbull of Whitby, Richardson Duck and
their neighbours Craig Taylor of Stockton.

The company of Evan Thomas Radcliffe, one of the
largest in southern Wales, with its origins in Aber-porth
in Ceredigion, preferred ships from the Sunderland
area, in particular those of Bartram & Co., and of John
Blumer and Joseph Thompson, as well as occasional
vessels from the Tyne and the Clyde.

Since the tramp steamers of southern Wales
depended to a large extent on the coal industry for their
livelihood, shipping companies were very unwilling to
use any fuel other than coal to power their ships at a
time when almost all shipowners in the rest of Europe
had adopted oil as their fuel. One individual who
ventured into the area of motor ships was Owen
Williams from the Edern district, who built the
Margretian in 1923. A year later this was followed by the
Silurian. Both ships proved to be extremely unpopular,
and between 1923 and 1930 *Cwmni Llongau Pwllparc*
[Pwllparc Shipping Company] made a staggering loss
of £400,000 and the firm was wound up in 1930. Until

she was laid up, the oil-fired *Margretian* was just as unpopular in Cardiff between 1925 and 1929.

By the 1960s, the entire shipbuilding industry in Britain was waning, and nowadays it is ships from Korea and Japan, Turkey and Romania that we see in our ports.

If steamship builders were uncommon in Wales, this was not the case with regard to ship repair companies. Dry dock facilities were considered to be essential to the activities of any busy port. In south Wales, the following dry docks were operating in 1960:

CARDIFF
Commercial Dry Dock	Length 600 feet
Gridiron	Length 250 feet
Channel	Length 635 feet
Mountstuart 1	Length 600 feet
Mountstuart 2	Length 430 feet
Mountstuart 3	Length 495 feet
Junction	Length 413 feet
East Dry Dock 1	Length 408 feet
East Dry Dock 2	Length 400 feet
Bute West Graving Dock	Length 235 feet

PENARTH
Floating Pontoon	Length 415 feet

NEWPORT
Commercial Dry Dock	Length 523 feet
Tredegar Dry Dock	Length 712 feet
Bailey's Dry Dock	Length 454 feet

BARRY
Bailey's Dry Dock	Length 940 feet
Graving Dock No. 1	Length 795 feet
Graving Dock No. 2	Length 620 feet

PORT TALBOT
Graving Dock   Length 460 feet

SWANSEA
Commercial Dry Dock   Length 263 feet
Duke of Edinburgh Dry Dock   Length 670 feet
Palmers' Dry Dock   Length 560 feet
Prince of Wales Dry Dock   Length 455 feet
South Dry Dock (for Fishing Craft)   Length 170 feet

In the west, the dry dock at Milford Haven is still in operation, but the naval dry docks at Pembroke Dock are now gone. In northern Wales, Y Felinheli and Holyhead both had dry docks, and it was possible to drag ships onto dry land by using the patent slip in Victoria Dock in Caernarfon.

Compared to the bustle of the past, the ports of Wales are now very quiet and ships rarely visit those places that were once a frenzy of activity. The tradition has died and it is doubtful that it will ever return.

Shipowners

Until about the last quarter of the nineteenth century, ships provided the main form of transport in Wales. With poor roads, and the railway network not yet fully developed, ships were vital for the import of essential commodities and for the export of farm, quarry and mine products. Until the end of the nineteenth century, almost every coastal community had its fleet of small sailing ships, which provided their main link with the rest of the outside world. Many of these little ships were constructed locally, and in Ceredigion, Llŷn and Anglesey, for example, a large number of vessels were owned by the ship's master himself. Occasionally, the master would perhaps have only one or two shares in his ship, and the rest would be in the hands of people who were not sailors. Farmers in particular were often multiple shareholders in local ships, as it was beneficial for them to own a means of transporting fertiliser for their land and fuel for their homes, and to avail themselves of the best means of exporting agricultural produce. In many villages, traders were responsible for importing goods to coastal towns or villages and for their distribution in the surrounding countryside.

A good example is the small village of Llangrannog in Ceredigion, which – at that time if not today – was typical of the small coastal hamlets of western Wales. The sea originally brought Crannog, the Celtic missionary who established the original settlement in the sixth century A.D., and it is mainly the sea that attracts all sorts of visitors in the twenty-first century. It was around the middle of the eighteenth century that maritime traffic became established in the area. Unfortunately, according to Howell Harris, a leading Methodist, it was an unpleasant place: 'a dark country . . . and that better fall amongst thieves than here', because smuggling was common in the local population. Nevertheless, by 1750 seafaring was an important component of the life of the district, with families from the surrounding countryside opting to settle at the water's edge. The first dwelling to be established in this way was Eisteddfa House, which was built by John Griffiths from the nearby farm of the same name. He set up a shipping company close to Llangrannog beach, and within a few years, he owned eight small ships. There were others, such as my own great-great-grandfather, Captain Joseph Jenkins (1820-1904), one of the stalwarts of the Bancyfelin Methodist chapel as well as of the Pentre Arms, who moved from the Penbryn area some three miles away to establish a business involving four ships. Between 1787 and 1859 a total of fifteen ships were built near the beach, varying in size from the 7-ton smack *Linnet*, which was built in 1824, to the 211-ton brig *Ann Catherine*, which was built in 1859. Apart from the ships that were built locally, the businessmen of Llangrannog were also quite prepared to buy ships from other builders. There was Daniel Davies, for example, who bought a brigantine of 130 tons, the *Hawendale*, from New Quay in 1858, and John Owen who, in the same year, bought an 158-ton brig, the *Ada Letitia* from Sunderland. Of course, from around 1850 onwards, most of the ships belonging to Llangrannog shipowners sailed far and wide, although the company offices remained in Llangrannog. Naturally, up until the end of the nineteenth century, the small ships with their cargoes of *cwlwm* and coal, lime and crockery, would still come to the village. In fact some forty ships were owned by people from Llangrannog up until the last twenty years of the nineteenth century. With the advent of the railway to Cardigan in 1880 and to Newcastle Emlyn in 1895, the ownership of vessels in the village declined. The businessmen of Llangrannog showed no interest whatsoever in steamships until at least 1928, when Captain William George James of Ivy House, Llangrannog, and his brother-in-law, Captain William Davies of Angorfa, Llangrannog, established the *British Isles Coasters Ltd*, a company which enjoyed some success until about 1940. Of course, none of their ships ever saw the beach at Llangrannog, and the head office was in Cardigan. They ran a total of eight small ships, employing crews from Llangrannog. The lives of these sailors was decidely uncomfortable.

In the boom days of the nineteenth century, a large number of local inhabitants were able to hold shares in ships. For example, listed below are the shareholders of the brig *Ann Catherine*, a ship measuring some 193 feet in length, 25 feet in breadth and 13.6 feet in height, which was built on the beach at Llangrannog in the 1850s:

James Lloyd – Master Mariner	14 shares
Evan Lloyd – Master Mariner	2 shares
Catherine Lloyd, New Inn – Spinster	2 shares
John Davies, New Inn – Innkeeper	2 shares
Josiah Jones, Pontgarreg – Shopkeeper	2 shares
John Patrick, New Quay – Innkeeper	2 shares
John Davies, New Quay – Master Mariner	2 shares
Thomas Davies, New Quay – Blacksmith	1 share
David Davies, New Quay – Blacksmith	1 share
Thomas Davies, Penbryn – Farmer	2 shares
Daniel Rees, Penparc – Farmer	2 shares
Dd Jones, Dyffryn Bern, Tre-saith, Farmer	2 shares
Elias Jones, Blaenhownant Isaf – Farmer	2 shares
David Jones, Cefnceirw – Farmer	2 shares
Daniel Owen, Fronfelen – Farmer	2 shares
John Evans, Pantygronglwyd – Farmer	6 shares
Mary Evans, Capel Gwnda – Widow	4 shares

Hannah Lloyd, Cwmbarre – Widow	1 share
Samuel Lewis, Rhydlewis – Tanner	4 shares
Henry Lloyd, Llwynteg – Joiner	2 shares
Thomas Edwards, Cardigan – Merchant	4 shares
William Davies, Glanesger	2 shares
Thomas Lewis, Aberdare	2 shares

With a crew of nine, all of them from the village of Llangrannog, the *Ann Catherine* sailed far and wide under the captaincy of two masters – the Business Master, John Lloyd, from the Ship Inn, who did not hold a master's certificate, and Evan Lloyd, the Sailing Master. The ship enjoyed some success until it was wrecked near Aberffraw in Anglesey in 1876.

It was the steamships, of course, which killed off much of the activity of the shipowners in the most rural parts of Wales. Of the thirty-seven owners controlling some eighty-nine ships out of their offices in New Quay, Ceredigion, in 1865, for example, all had disappeared by 1900. Thus, even in the last days of the sailing ships, there was an attempt on the part of several shipowners in western and northern Wales to prevent the decline in their prosperity by purchasing ships from north America – from Quebec and Prince Edward Island – and sailing them across the world. The ships that sailed from the big ports throughout the world were extremely graceful. They never visited the coastal villages that were home to the companies' head offices, and it was only a matter of time before the most ambitious of these companies moved their offices to the large ports – to Cardiff and Liverpool in particular. This era came to an end, although the maritime tradition in rural areas still survived for a short while.

As the size of the ships increased, the activity of the numerous small ports decreased throughout Wales. With the transition from sail to steam, the major ports became the magnet for the mariners of Wales. Large numbers of them moved to the big ports: some went to the ports of Tyne and Clyde, but the majority of them headed for two of the largest ports – Liverpool in the case of sailors from northern Wales, and Cardiff, and to a lesser extent Swansea, for the sailors of western Wales. Numerous families moved from the countryside and set up home in the cities. As they were familiar with working on small vessels along the treacherous Irish Sea coast, the sailors of rural Wales were in great demand to serve on ships trading from the major ports.

'To procure another master,' stated one tramp steamer owner from Cardiff,

> we have to look to the West, for here in Cardiff there is not one that can be trusted with such a vessel and such a trade as may be found in Sunderland, London and Bristol. Cardiff masters are confined to the coastal trade in a very narrow sphere and I feel that most of them are so deficient in that kind of distinction between mayhem and tohem as to make them ineligible.

This was praise indeed, and it is not surprising that a shipping company such as Evan Thomas Radcliffe attracted the majority of the masters and their officers from the villages of Aber-porth, Llangrannog, Llandudoch and Nanhyfer during the golden age prior to the First World War, when the company owned some thirty-five steamships which traded throughout the world. Smaller companies which owned ships that sailed from remote ports also moved to Cardiff.

In the same way that Cardiff acted as a magnet to sailors and shipowners from western Wales during the second half of the nineteenth century, Liverpool attracted mariners from northern Wales. From Anglesey and Arfon, Merioneth and Denbigh, thousands went to work in this huge metropolis on the banks of the Mersey. With a host of chapels and Welsh-speaking societies, Liverpool was the true capital of northern Wales. With enormous companies such as the *Black Ball Line* and *Alfred Holt* employing so many from Wales, the Holt Line – *The Blue Funnel Line* – came to be known as 'the Welsh Navy'. This company was formed in 1865 and it was common for the women of Llŷn to take a son who was keen on becoming a seaman to see Lawrence Holt at his summer residence, in an attempt to get him signed up on one of the company's numerous steamships.

Chapel society was very important on the banks of the Mersey. 'The spirit of the times in the 19th century,' observed Alan Scarth from the Liverpool Museum, 'was to marry honesty with business. Chapels formed a network. Going to church was not only a religious experience.' The same attitude was also to be found among the shipowners of Cardiff, with many of them active in nonconformist chapels, such as the Calvinistic chapels of Salem and Pembroke Terrace, and the Independent chapels of Ebeneser and Frederick Street. Many Welsh shipowners sprang from families known for religious and business zeal. The marine historian Aled Eames went as far as to write that such men were often associated with incredible meanness and that they sat piously in their chapels and shook their heads when they heard the complaints and tragedies relating to their ships and to the men whose toil brought them the profits that enabled them to build their fine houses and many chapels.

It should not be forgotten that Liverpool, like Bristol, was one of the main centres for the slave trade, until the trade was made illegal. Liverpool was also the main port for emigration from Britain – emigration in ships that were often both difficult to handle and unhealthy. Imbued with confidence, hope and endless dreams of a better world, the emigrants would put all their faith in the agents, some of whom were honest, others who were not, to arrange a passage to north and south America and Australia. Bill Jones observed that:

> Rail links helped with emigrant trains leaving from South Wales for Liverpool every Monday. Many migrants used emigration agents who themselves had representatives in Welsh towns. Some agents were reported to be unreliable or tricksters, so much so that in the 1870's the emigration agent Gomer Roberts promised in his newspaper advertisements to meet his customers sober and to put them on the right ship.

A number of Welsh people form northern Wales took advantage of this trade, and although various large shipping companies, such as Davies from Menai Bridge, ran an enormous enterprise with global links from their offices in Anglesey, there were others who were only too willing to move to Liverpool. For example, shipping companies from Gwynedd, such as William Thomas & Co, 30 Brunswick Street and 14 Water Street, Liverpool, with forty-four large ships to their name – both sail and steam – had their offices in Liverpool during the last quarter of the nineteenth century. Or there was Richard Thomas, of Cricieth and Richmond Buildings Liverpool, who owned thirty-three ships between 1878 and 1907.

With other companies such as Roberts, Owen & Co, 19 Oldfield Street (who owned twelve ships) and several much smaller operators, shipowners from Wales were an important element in the business life of the Liverpool docks.

The history of Cardiff as an international port was equally exciting. A large number of shipowners established companies here to carry coal and iron from the south of Wales to all parts of the world. As in the case of Liverpool, which depended heavily on seamen from the remotest corners of northern Wales, Cardiff too attracted new shipowners from all over the British Isles following its spectacular growth in the second half of the nineteenth century. Until the 1850s, Cardiff was a fairly insignificant place: some coal and iron was exported from the landing-stages on the Afon Taf near the castle, in sailing ships that belonged to businessmen from elsewhere – such as Bristol. In fact, until the mid-nineteenth century, other ports like Aberystwyth and Cardigan had more ships than Cardiff. In 1850, Cardiff had just sixty-eight sailing ships, but during the ensuing twenty years, the number of steamships owned by Cardiff increased with phenomenal speed. Among the early owners were:

> *William Cory* from Hartland in Devon together with *John Nixon*, the coalowner who bought the *S.S. William Cory* (1168 tons) from a yard on the Tyne in 1857.

> *H. Vellacott* who built the *S.S. Llandaff* (411 tons) in 1865 and the *S.S. Fairwater* a year later.

> *Charles Stallybrass*, born in Siberia in 1838 and who came to Cardiff in 1857 and built the *S.S. Leckwith* in 1868.

These three individuals, all immigrants to Cardiff, were the true pioneers of its docks, and soon they were followed by others. Cardiff was developing very rapidly as one of the most important ports in the country; it attracted thousands of sailors and dockers, all kinds of shopkeepers, and hundreds involved in the night-time entertainment of this most colourful of European ports. The shipowners came from all parts:

the Morel Brothers from Jersey, for example, together with J.B. Hacquoil and H.B. Marquand. Many came from western England – individuals such as John Cory; his cousins, John and Richard, [the Cory brothers] from Appledore; John Angel Gibbs from Portland; W.J. Tatem from Appledore, and William Reardon Smith, also from Appledore.

A number of Welshmen set up business in the Cardiff docks and became particularly important as shipowners. From the small village of Aber-porth in Ceredigion came the two brothers-in-law, James and David Jenkins, who joined forces with a shipping clerk from Bethesda in 1898 to set up a business with seven ships . Some who were less successful came from the same village – such as Capt. Thomas Owen and Henry Bartlett, who established the *Glanhowny Steamship Company* in 1903 and who went bankrupt within four years when their only ship the *Glanhowny* was lost. Another failure was Daniel Jenkins, of Bryntirion, Aber-porth, whose only ship – the *S.S. Aberporth* – was lost in suspicious circumstances in the Black Sea in 1905, less than two years after it had been bought.

The most successful of all the Cardiff shipping companies originating in Aber-porth was that of Evan Thomas: Evan was the son of Hezekiah Thomas, a smallholder from Dolwen, Aber-porth who owned a small ketch, the *Pheasant*. With Henry Radcliffe from Merthyr Tydfil Evan built up the largest of the shipping companies in Cardiff. By 1914, this company had as many as thirty-five ships, a large number of them crewed by masters, officers and seamen from western Wales. Owen, Evan and David Owen's family came from Y Foel, a farm in the remote area between Llangrannog and New Quay, not far from the lonely beach of Cwmtydu. They tried their luck in Cardiff during the dark days of the First World War and continued to work there until 1933. The name chosen for this company with its offices in Imperial Buildings, Cardiff, was a strange one: the *Anglo Belgique Shipping Company Ltd*.

Another with a penchant for fancy names was John Mathias, the grocer from Stryd y Bont in Aberystwyth, who moved to Cardiff around 1905. He named his ships after public schools such as Harrow and Rugby, although the ships were known as *Llongau Aberystwyth* in everyday parlance. He named the company, which began unremarkably enough in 1875 in Aberystwyth, the *College Line*. John Mathias was an elder in the influential Tabernacl chapel in Aberystwyth, and a number of his fellow elders and its well-known minister, the Reverend Thomas Levi, together with the first Principal of the university at Aberystwyth were investors in this company. Captains from Aberystwyth and Y Borth were the main employees of the company, which failed in 1924.

Another Cardiff shipping company was set up by the Owen brothers and Watkin Williams, who came from the village of Edern in Llŷn. Their ships were known as *Llongau Pwll Parc*, after their home in Edern.

Apart from the Welsh, Cardiff attracted all sorts of ambitious shipowners, both honest and dishonest, and in 1920 the port was home to as many as a hundred and twenty-two shipping companies. But there were difficult days ahead, and by 1931 seventy-seven companies owning a total of three hundred and thirteen ships were left. By 1939, only fifty-seven companies remained, and in 2005 there were just two left in a port which, at one time, was considered to be the 'greatest steamship owning centre in the world'.

Of course it was not particularly difficult to become a shipowner in a big port like Cardiff, and although a considerable number were financed by the old system of 64-shares per ship, after the Companies Act of 1862 it was possible to finance shipping companies on the Stock Exchange, and a ship could have hundreds of investors who knew nothing about the sea or its ships. Nevertheless, for many the old system persisted. In this system, four shares were described as an ounce of a ship. Men like Evan Thomas and Henry Radcliffe only ventured to purchase a single share, worth some £270, in their first ship, the *Gwenllian Thomas*, in 1882. The remaining shareholders – none of whom owned more than two shares – came from all over the country: from Dolgellau, Aber-porth, Pen-y-bont, Corwen, Cardiff and Y Bala. The *Gwenllian* only cost £17,000 from the *Palmer Shipbuilding and Iron Company* yard, which was in Jarrow on the river Tyne. As a result of the company's terrific growth over the subsequent ten years, investors had to be attracted from further afield.

It was essential not only for the shipping companies of Cardiff but also those of Swansea, Menai Bridge, Porthmadog and even Liverpool, to see investment from all over the country. Between 1880 and 1922, becoming an investor in a ship could mark the onset of a madcap career for many – for schoolmasters, quarrymen, dozens of Methodist ministers, farmers and flannel manufacturers. The investors did stand to receive a small amount of the profits, but there were also devastating losses, with some very promising companies going under and failing to pay a single farthing to their investors.

'We are absolutely without funds,' complained one owner of the *Glanhowny* in 1909: 'there is not one penny with which to do anything.' The investment of a number of families from western Wales disappeared with the failure of the company.

There was also the case of Edgar Edwards, from Llandaf – an optimist if ever there was one. In

December 1918 he bought all the ships belonging to Sir Walter Runciman of Newcastle for £1.8 million. Runciman was wise enough to realise that there were difficult times ahead and he was fortunate enough to unload his entire fleet on a Welshman from Cardiff who was ambitious but incompetent. Despite a further £2 million investment in 1920, by 1922, Edwards and his *Western Counties Shipping Co. Ltd* were in all sorts of trouble. By April 1922 the end came, and Edgar Edwards went bankrupt.

Unfortunately, with the disappearance of so many ships and owners in the 1920s, the investments and hopes of a great many ordinary people also disappeared. Worst of all, during this difficult period, many of the owners also vanished with money that belonged to schoolmasters, widows and Methodist preachers who had looked forward to a considerable income from their capital.

The process of setting up these shipping companies in the big ports around Britain in the nineteenth century involved establishing what was known as a *Single Ship Company*. The establishment of a new company did not require a great deal of money from the prospective owner of the company. As Robin Craig observes:

> The limited joint stock company and especially the single ship company became the means to ensure the capitalisation of an ever expanding fleet. Therefore for every vessel there could be hundreds of shareholders, some of them investing only a few pounds in a ship. In the good years dividends went high but in bad years disaster could face the small investor who had staked his life savings in a shipping company. The person who really profited from operating a single ship company was the

manager, the person who had floated the company; very often he had little financial stake in a company, but he took a commission of gross earnings rather than on profits, so that provided he was getting a freight he was not gravely concerned with the profitability of the Company's operation.

This entirely legal system of funding had its advantages, since it was easy to raise capital by publicising the spectacular results of some companies in the press. It was a simple matter to persuade people to invest in immediate success. Between 1882 and 1913, the renowned company of Evan Thomas Radcliffe operated its whole fleet under single ship companies; the company was at its largest when the first thirty-one ships were built between 1882 and 1908. Following the large-scale losses of the First World War, when twenty ships were sunk, the system was fairly acceptable to the owners.

Of course, during the golden age of the ports, it was important that the shipping companies had people who were prepared to promote new companies all over the country. Since ministers of religion travelled around so much, a number of shipowners took advantage of their peripatetic habits. For example, in Anglesey, the Reverend John Elias was an excellent ambassador for the Davies family from Menai Bridge, not only in terms of promoting the company's fortune throughout the country, but also in obtaining shares. Several chapels in Anglesey had been established with funds acquired from this notable and wealthy family. Funds from ships were also responsible for building a number of nonconformist chapels in Liverpool and Merseyside. In Cardiff, shipowners were responsible for funding Methodist chapels in Pembroke Terrace and Salem, Canton. Many prominent businessmen from the docks were elders in these establishments.

As already mentioned, in Aberystwyth, again, the influence of the Reverend Thomas Levi may be seen: the minister of the Tabernacl and a remarkable preacher, he was an investor in the company of one of the chapel elders, John Mathias.

But king among the maritime ministers was the Reverend John Cynddylan Jones (1840-1934). He was a true Cardi, and became minister of Frederick Street Church in Cardiff and the secretary of the Bible Society. Among the members of his congregation were Evan Thomas and Henry Radcliffe, although their membership was somewhat nominal. As one of the major problems for any new company during the last quarter of the nineteenth century was that of trying to raise capital, the minister saw his chance. Evan Thomas' brother-in-law, Jenkin David, the manager of the National Provincial in Dolgellau, did his best to persuade customers – farmers, quarrymen, preachers and schoolmasters and even Thomas Gee, the famous publisher from Denbigh – to invest. But the enterprise required far more capital than the savings of a few people from the north. Cynddylan was a fine preacher who was in demand all over of the country, and one of his main tasks was to persuade members of every congregation to invest. Thousands of pounds were invested through his efforts. According to *The Lighthouse* magazine in 1886:

> Messrs E. Thomas, Radcliffe & Co. obtained a recommendation from the Reverend J. Cynddylan Jones (who was, we believe, pastor of the chapel which H. Radcliffe patronises) to the effect that several of his friends had invested money with Messrs E. Thomas Radcliffe & Co. and were perfectly satisfied. This was very nice as the Rev.

Cynddylan Jones was and no doubt still is a kindly and highly respected minister of the Calvinistic Methodist connection. This recommendation besides in any cases being attached to the prospector was also inserted in a Welsh newspaper, circulating in North Wales where the Calvinistic Methodists are very strong. As a larger proportion of the shareholders of the *Anne Thomas* reside in North Wales, the revised gentleman's 'testimonial' apparently carried weight with it. We don't know of course that he had any particular motive in going out of his way to recommend ship owning, so presume that in doing so he only desired to do what he could to promote the welfare of his flock: but under any circumstances he deserved to be appointed Chaplain to the Fleet, that is presuming the fleet required a Chaplain.

Cynddylan was motivated not so much by the spiritual well-being of his congregation, as by the fact that the eloquent preacher stood to receive two per cent of the profits of the total number of single ship concerns under the company's umbrella – a very considerable sum of money, when one bears in mind that the company owned fifteen ships within ten years of its establishment. By 1889, the pastor was dissatisfied with his lot and tried to claim two shares in every ship. His application was turned down and matters became quite unpleasant: Cynddylan planted the idea among the investors from north Wales (probably on one of his frequent preaching tours) that they were not receiving the income which was due to them. Matters became very turbulent, with strong-worded articles in *Y Genedl* [The Nation] and public meetings in places such as Llanrwst. With the death of Evan Thomas in 1891, Cynddylan strove to ensure that he was succeeded as chairman of the Company by his brother Thomas Thomas, a farmer from Dolwen, Aber-porth. His attempt to turn matters in his favour was unsuccessful, but under the presidency of the brothers Henry and Daniel Radcliffe, the company became one of the most prosperous ever in south Wales.

Although the railway and improved state of the roads in general depleted much of the maritime trade towards the end of the nineteenth century, there were still a number of shipping companies trading into the next century. The most notable of these, perhaps, were the companies which still carried a variety of cargoes to remote ports in rural Wales. For example, although the splendour of the port of Caernarfon was gone by 1900, five grocers in the town decided to establish the *Carnarvon and Liverpool Steamship Co.* Initially, in 1893, they acquired a small steamer called the *Ibis* and, subsequently, the *S.S. Christianna*. The company competed with the *Liverpool, Carnarvon and Menai Straits Steamship Co.* and its ship the *Prince Jaja* until it merged with them in 1901.

Despite all the competition, some companies remained in operation until the 1930s. For example, James Davies from Cardigan kept going with his little ship the *S.S. Teifi*, and likewise Captain John Davies of Maesteg, Y Borth, Ceredigion with the *Plas Dinam* until it was wrecked in Canada, and the *Therese*, which ended its days on Goodwin sands. Perhaps the last of the Welsh captain-owners was John George from Trefin in Pembrokeshire, who carried on sailing the *S.S. Ben Rein* along the coast of Wales until 1936.

Trade

Although Wales had a number of ports in the Middle Ages, most of these were the creation of conquering foreign powers. Most of the mariners sailing along the coast were foreigners too, because the medieval Welsh were no great seamen, and were unable to venture very far off shore. The majority of the Welsh ports were landing places for the Norman invaders, and these ports grew up in the shadow of the Norman castles. For example, in the west, the main ports of Carmarthen Bay were Cydweli, Carmarthen, Talacharn and, in particular, Tenby – ports originally established to meet the needs of the occupants of the castle. Over the years, a maritime trade developed from these medieval ports: wool and animal skins in particular were exported, usually to France and Spain, and fruit and wine were imported. With the development of fisheries the medieval ports became quite busy, and maritime trade became a profitable source of income for the merchants of the seaboard boroughs.

Apart from the trade associated with the castles, there was a good deal of maritime activity elsewhere in medieval Wales, where remote beaches provided a landing for ships from other regions. In the Bristol Channel, for example, ships from Bristol, Somerset and Devon would visit on a regular basis, and there were river landings, such as at Caerleon and Chepstow, which were quite important ports, distributing a variety of goods to a large rural hinterland. In Glamorgan there was a landing near the castle at Cardiff on the Afon Taf, and there were also landings on the coast of the Vale of Glamorgan – at Barry, Sully, Aberddawan (Aberthaw) and Ogwr. A wide range of commodities from wine to red bricks, brought in ships from the west of England, would arrive on the nearest beach, and agricultural produce in particular would be exported. These primitive harbours were entirely unsuitable for the export of coal and iron, which was to become so important in the economic history of Wales at a later date.

Prior to the Acts of Union in 1536, the coast of Pembroke and Cardigan Bay were fairly perilous places for sailors because of piracy, which was endemic in these parts, and all types of ships were at risk of attack. Subsequently, an attempt was made to improve the situation and to curb their activities.

Up until the end of the seventeenth century, fishing, particularly for herring, was extremely important in the west. The Royal Commission, which came to western Wales to conduct a survey of the maritime resources, observed in 1565 that:

> they possessed no ships barks or vessels of any kind but certain fisher boats of the burthen of 4 or 5 tons at the most and these maintained by poor fishermen for the only use and exercise of fishing.

It was probably part-time fishermen and farmers who were responsible for going after the herring between the beginning of September and the middle of December every year. In addition to the fish sold locally, the export of red and salted herring became a major industry. It was primarily Irish boats that were involved in its export, and vessels from Dublin and Wexford and other Irish ports were regular visitors to Fishguard in the south, right up to Aberystwyth and Aberdyfi in the north. Most of the paraphernalia of the fishing trade also had to be imported, such as barrels and nets, and especially salt. Since salt was a good deal cheaper in Ireland than in Wales, it was one of the most common and important commodities to be smuggled, at the dead of night, on to the western beaches. In

August 1704, for example, this report appears in a local paper:

> The Aberdovey Customs Officers suspecting an iminent [sic] landing of contraband salt went to New Quay at 3 a.m. to find three boats full of salt near the shore and above a hundred and fifty men and two hundred horses on the shore ready to carry it away.

Salt was so essential for fishermen and farmers alike that, in addition to the salt from Ireland, much of it came from Lancashire and Cheshire, especially to ports north of Aberystwyth.

Several businessmen from Ireland settled in Wales. Patrick Brown, for example, who became a shipowner, arrived from Ireland, married a woman from the well-known farm of Mabws Fawr, near St. David's, and established a business in the town of Cardigan.

In the north, the region's long coastline depended for trade on ships from Liverpool, Deeside, Fleetwood and other ports in the north-west of England, and Welsh sailors were few and far between until the eighteenth century. But by the mid-eighteenth century the Welsh were no longer such landlubbers and had begun to take an interest in maritime trade, which, up until that time, had been the monopoly of others. The Welsh mariner had arrived, and an increasing number of Welsh ships now sailed along the Welsh coast. It was the 1800s that saw the real establishment of the Welsh maritime tradition, which was to become so important in the lives of the coastal towns, villages and areas from the mouth of the Afon Gwy in the south right up to the Deeside in the north.

In Ceredigion, for example, my great-great-grandfather, David Jenkins of Plasbach, Penbryn, a smallholder and part-time fisherman, was sufficiently enterprising in 1777 to become a partner in the building of a small 24-ton sloop called the *Blessing*. She was built not far from the open beach of Penbryn, and he sailed her as far as Ireland with a cargo of salt herring and barrels of butter. He found himself a wife in the town of Wicklow – my great-great-grandmother, Hannah Christmas. For some time he farmed a smallholding, fished, and sailed to Ireland. His son Joseph (1820-1904) had no interest whatsoever in working on the land – he was a full-time sailor throughout his life. The port of Llangrannog was his home from about 1850 onwards, and there he brought up four boys and three girls. The sons were all sailors, as was the husband of one of the daughters. For a family who depended on the sea for a living it was a tragic life:

John (1852-1885) – drowned near Rio de Janeiro

James (1853-1887) – drowned on a voyage from Java to Queenstown

Joseph (1855-1893) – drowned near the Scilly Isles on a voyage from Valparaiso to Cardiff

David (1850-1894) – died in Llangrannog

Joseph's sons sailed far and wide, of course, travelling the world in comparatively large ships, many of which belonged to shipowners from New Quay.

This vital activity was at its height in the nineteenth century, when sailors and ships from Wales sailed all over the world. Their contribution to the rich tradition and qualities of Wales as a nation has been invaluable.

Sailing the coasts

Before the mid-nineteenth century, however, coastal rather than ocean sailing was the main occupation for Welsh sailors, although there was a considerable amount of traffic between Wales and continental Europe, America and the rest of the world. Essential commodities for coastal communities would arrive at the beaches in small ships, many of which were built locally and were specially designed to lie flat on the sand of an open beach. Everything the community needed was carried in hundreds of such small craft which were usually crewed by a master, a mate and a ship's boy. Lime for fertiliser, slates and bricks, fuel and building materials for the ports were brought in, and local agricultural produce or the product of local quarries was exported. Over time, Welsh sailors became more adventurous: the ports of France, Spain and the Mediterranean were within reach of the schooners that were becoming increasingly popular with Welsh merchant traders.

As the years went by, regular services for passengers and goods were established in many parts of the country. Ships from Liverpool and Lancashire made regular runs to the ports of northern Wales. From the ports of Cardigan Bay, such as Aberystwyth, Aberdyfi and Aberaeron, there was a regular service with Liverpool and ports in Ireland, as there was between the ports of Pembroke and Carmarthenshire and Bristol and London.

Many of the small ports exported regional products, although in most of Wales, imports and the transporting of goods from other ports of Wales were much more significant than exports. In the days of the small sailing ships, a number of these harbours were extremely important. For example, the ports of southern Pembrokeshire and Carmarthen Bay, such as Hook and Pembrey, exported *cwlwm*, the main fuel for the homes of western Wales as far north as Aberaeron. In south Pembrokeshire ports such as Lydstep, Stackpole and Caldey Island transported limestone to be burnt in the lime kilns that were to be seen along the whole length of the Welsh coast. On the western coast of Pembrokeshire there were ports such as Porth-gain, which had been specifically developed to export Abereiddi granite. Of course, the ports of the Bristol Channel exported coal long before the extraordinary developments of the latter half of the nineteenth century, while a number of ports in the north had evolved to export specific products. For example, the development of Barmouth was closely linked with the Meirionnydd wool trade, while slates were exported from particular ports such as Porthmadog, Caernarfon, Y Felinheli and Bangor, and copper from Amlwch to Swansea.

Sailing the ocean

Gradually, as the railway network reached even the most isolated of Welsh coastal areas, the demand for small ships carrying essential commodities along the coast to remote communities declined. Many of the sloops and schooners that had been such a common sight throughout Wales began to disappear, and several of the masters of small ships and their owners gave up their business. In fact, in order for the sailors and owners to survive, their interests had to expand from the coasts of Britain and Western Europe to every part of the world. Larger ships had to be purchased – ships that could sail to distant parts of the world. In time, it became cheaper to buy large sailing ships from overseas, particularly from the banks of the St Lawrence in New England and Prince Edward Island in Canada.

For example, New Quay had a number of such ships in the years between 1865 and 1880:

> *Ann Ramsey*, barque, 407 tons. Built Quebec 1863.
> *Susannah Kemp*, brig, 178 tons. Built Prince Edward Island (PEI) 1863.
> *Walter I. Cummins*, brig, 144 tons. Built New Brunswick 1865.
> *Derby*, brig, 257 tons. Built PEI 1868.
> *Resolven*, brig, 143 tons. Built PEI 1873.
> *Adela S. Hills*, barque 463 tons. Built Rockland Virginia 1874.
> *Maggie Cummins*, brig 293 tons. Built PEI 1873.
> *Pearl*, brigantine, 145 tons. Built PEI 1875.
> *Adriene*, brigantine, 145 tons. Built PEI 1875.
> *Lynwood*, brigantine, 175 tons. Built PEI 1875.
> *Raymond*, brigantine, 188 tons. Built PEI 1876.
> *Hero*, barque, 369 tons. Built PEI 1876.

Although none of these large sailing ships ever visited the ports in the villages of northern and western Wales where their owners resided, the company offices remained in the villages, and sailors from the area would be employed as crew. For example, the large company run by the Davies family never left its offices in Menai Bridge, and the administration of their fleet of big ships, which traded all over the world, was organised from that location. A number of the old shipmasters of New Quay adhered stubbornly to that port as the centre for their activities. Individuals such as John Phillips, Y Glyn (whose family was known as 'The Foxes') still worked six comparatively large vessels in 1875, while his neighbour, David Davies, ran four big sailing ships. Among these were the *Hetty Elen*, an 189-ton brig built in Llanelli in 1860. Under the captaincy of Captain David Davies from New Quay and a crew of nine – seven from Cei, one Irishman and one Scotsman – the ship was secured by Mr Rae, the agent of Dr David Livingstone, to carry all the missionary's supplies and Mrs Livingstone to West Luada on the Zambezi, arriving there on the 8th of January, 1862. From there the *Hetty Elen* sailed to Mauritius to take on a cargo of sugar for Bristol. Aled Eames observes:

> Almost every sailor from Wales in the age of sail was very familiar with a number of overseas ports, such as Hamburg and Antwerp, in Europe; Callao and Iquiquqe in western south America; San Francisco and Portland Oregon, and certainly Melbourne, Sydney, Adelaide and Newcastle, New South Wales. . . . To the sailors from the coasts of Wales, names such as 'Frisco, Portland Oregon, Port Phillip Heads, Williamstown, Sydney, Chinchas and Luboi d'Afuerra, Coquimbo and Cape Horn were more familiar than Llanbryn-mair or Y Bala.

Although ships in the latter half of the nineteenth century were large and carried many sails, there were also much smaller ships sailing the ocean. On the long voyages to Australia or California it was to the trader's advantage if the voyage was completed as quickly as possible. In January 1889, for example, the 1468-ton *Merioneth*, a ship belonging to Davies of Menai Bridge, reached San Francisco from Cardiff in ninety-six days with a cargo of Welsh coal. The master was Captain Robert Thomas from Llandwrog, and many of the crew were from northern Wales. Very often the voyage from Britain to California could take five months. The voyages of large sailing ships from Australia and the Far East, which brought wool and tea back home, were legendary, and the achievements of ships belonging to Welsh owners were just as important as the *Cutty Sark* and the *Thermopylae*. One might mention, among others, the *City of Melbourne* under the command of Captain Richard Jones of Caernarfon, which completed a passage from Australia in seventy-three days, or the *Lightning* under Captain Henry Jones from Menai Bridge, which completed a voyage from Melbourne to London in sixty-nine days. A number of captains from Wales were renowned for the speed of their sailing ships, and it seems more than likely that the majority of the crews on ships such as the *Whirlwind* and the *Royal Oak*, the *Lightning* and the *Empress of the Sea*, were men from rural north Wales. Alan Villiers, a world authority on the big sailing ships remarks:

> Take all the Lloyds, Llewelyns, Lewises, Hugheses, Davieses, Williamses, Owenses, Jenkinses – or only the Joneses – from the British merchant service and more than half of it would come to a full stop. Considerably more than half the Cape Horn ships would not have sailed.

Apart from the long voyages where speed was crucial, there were other voyages where it was not such an important factor. Although steamships had replaced sail by the last quarter of the nineteenth century, the age of the sailing ships continued at least until 1916. Where the ships were designed to carry heavy cargoes, such as coal and iron and copper ore, speed was not so important. Many of these, like the ships of Swansea, had been built as cheaply as possible in America and Canada, and their losses – particularly when they were carrying copper ore from Chile – were staggering. The reputation of the ships and shipowners of Swansea was not particularly good. All kinds of ore was carried from all over of the world to meet the needs of the tinplate and steel furnaces of southern Wales, and it was in this trade that the sailing ships survived the longest.

One noteworthy trade, which employed a great many Welsh ships and sailors, was the guano trade from the Chincha Islands off the coast of Peru. There was a great demand for seabird droppings as an agricultural manure throughout Europe. Chinese labour was employed to break the rocks and load the ships and there were awful tales of the terrible hardship experienced by these immigrants under the iron rule of the quarry owners. A ship could wait weeks if not months before it was loaded with guano and it set sail on the dangerous voyage round Cape Horn. The Chinchas and the port of Callao were extremely unhealthy places. Nevertheless, it was a very profitable market and it is not surprising that the Davies family of Menai Bridge, who made their fortune by bringing guano from Peru to Britain, became known as 'the birdshit family'.

The main port for the guano trade was Callao, and the guano itself was described as:

> a strong manure about 20 per cent of the best being ammonia, which caused it to be very strong, so strong indeed that a person could not stay in the hold for more than two or three minutes.

Shovelling it off the terraces above the sea was extremely unhealthy and dangerous work, and it is not surprising that the Chinese – who, to all intents and purposes, were slaves – were very rarely able to complete their seven year agreed contract. One observer remarked:

> I often saw them getting whipped far worse than a horse is allowed to be whipped in England. Now indeed I have often seen it done out of bravado and

with no earthly need or excuse.

. . . It was pitiful to hear the poor fellows yelling.
These gaffers were generally their own countrymen
promoted and of course they must show what they
excelled in, namely cruelty.

In addition to the long wait in this most unhealthy and
remote anchorage, it was estimated that ninety days
were needed to load up every ship. It is not surprising
that a voyage from Britain to Callao and back could
take a year or longer.

During the nineteenth century, there was one other
market of considerable importance to Welsh sailors,
namely the regular trade of carrying salted and dried
cod from Labrador and Newfoundland to countries
bordering the Mediterranean. Comparatively small
ships would leave Porthmadog with a cargo of slates
for Canada, for example, and then would sail from
there with fish to Spain, Portugal or Italy. They would
return from the Mediterranean with wine, fruit, iron
ore or zinc to Wales or England, before returning again
to north America.

Steamships

The sailing ships continued to make long-distance
passages, but for shorter journeys, in which ships did
not have to be refuelled – the 'bunkers' – steam rapidly
replaced sail. With coaling stations in many parts of the
world, steamships were on the increase from 1850. In
Liverpool, for example, Alfred Holt's company
changed to steam in the 1860s, and in Cardiff,
steamships became very common after about 1857,
when a new steamship, the *William Cory*, was built by
the coalowner John Nixon and William Cory from

Devon. From 1870 onwards, ships from southern Wales exported south Wales coal to all parts of the world. Much of it was exported to the coaling stations scattered across the globe. By then, it was becoming daily more feasible for steamships to sail world-wide since they were able to refuel in designated ports. Much of the product of the coalfields of south Wales was exported to Mediterranean ports – to Genoa and Gibraltar, to Alexandria and Port Said, for example, where ships of the Royal and Merchant Navies were able to take on fuel. Ships from southern Wales would sail with coal to Mediterranean ports, then in ballast to the Black Sea – to Romania and the Crimea and ports such as Odessa and Novorosisk. Here they would pick up a cargo of grain for several ports in western Europe, particularly Hamburg, Rotterdam and Antwerp, before returning in ballast to Cardiff or Newport to load up with coal once again. All types of raw material, ore and timber, oil and fruit, would be imported through the ports of the Bristol Channel. After the First World War, the ports of south America became much more important to the ships of southern Wales than those of the Mediterranean and the Black Sea. In the 1920s in particular, Welsh ships would be regular visitors to places such as Buenos Aires and Rosario, Bahia Blanca and Montevideo. During the 1920s and 30s, ships from Wales – especially ships from Cardiff – sailed everywhere in the world, and Cardiff was considered to be the most important of all the "tramp steamer" ports in Britain.

Times changed, and there is now very little trade from Welsh ports. Newport is still in operation, but there are very few ships to be seen at Cardiff. Nowadays, the emphasis in Cardiff Bay is on leisure and recreation, rather than on the export of millions of tons of the best Welsh coal. Penarth, Porth-cawl and

Llansawel have all closed as ports, and things are pretty quiet in Barry and Swansea. In the west, only the oil terminal at Milford Haven remains, and were it not for the ferry to Rosslare, there would be nothing happening at Fishguard. In the north, Holyhead is still an important ferry port, but apart from a little activity in Bangor and a little bit more at Mostyn, not much maritime trade remains. The tradition of hundreds of years is well and truly dying.

The Sailor's Life

During their heyday, sailing ships were considered to be objects of great romantic beauty, and the sailors who served on them were thought to enjoy a life of luxury. But the truth of the matter is that sailing ships, still vital until the last quarter of the nineteenth century, were the most dangerous means of transport ever invented. The ships were at the mercy of the winds and currents; the voyages were prolonged and uncomfortable; the food was uninspiring and often inedible, and the conditions on board were as bad as those experienced in the worst city slums. Often the crew would live in the fo'csle – an extremely cramped space – in amongst rusty, wet anchor chains. On the majority of ships, the fo'csle lacked a table or chairs, and the sailors had nowhere to eat their unsavoury food. To sleep, they would either use canvas hammocks or wooden bunk beds squeezed one on top of the other, with perhaps as many as twenty berths within a very confined space. Mattresses consisted of a canvas bag stuffed with straw – the 'donkey's breakfast' – which would soon become dirty and uncomfortable. In all weathers sailors had to climb to the rigging high above the deck to trim the sails. Every item of clothing and every nook and cranny on board would be wet. It is difficult to imagine a less appealing life than that of a sailor.

My father, Captain D.J. Jenkins, went to sea at the age of twelve in 1897 on board the *Foxglove*, which sailed out of Cardiff to Valparaiso, under the command of Captain James Davies [Capten Twba] from Rhydlewis. He told me:

'I was employed as a cook and deckhand at 15 shillings a month. They'd employ any old Tom, Dick or Harry as cook. We lived in the fo'csle in the front of the ship – no seats, no table, just a wooden clothes chest to sit on. Food was scarce and unpleasant – hard tack and dry salted meat. The fo'csle also housed the windlass for the anchor and whenever the ship dropped anchor, red rust would get over everything. When we weighed anchor, the whole fo'csle would be covered in mud. When the ship was at anchor, the hawse pipes would be open and water would flow in under the beds. A 'slush' lamp would be used to light the fo'csle, a piece of wick attached to a cork, floating in a bowl of paraffin. Our main fare was bully beef and salt pork and hard tack biscuits full of weevils. We were given six pints of water a day, and that had to suffice for everything – for drinking, washing and shaving!'

Nevertheless, despite the dangers and miserable conditions with which the sailors had to contend, a life at sea was still a major attraction for young boys in coastal villages. In fact, they may not have had much choice in the matter, and although the maritime trade of the coastal villages of Wales had disappeared almost completely by the beginning of the twentieth century, young men were still drawn to the sea. In areas such as Ceredigion and Llŷn, the quality of life in the coastal villages was quite different from villages inland. In places like Llangrannog and Aber-porth in Ceredigion, Nefyn and Aberdaron in Llŷn and Moelfre and Amlwch in Anglesey, the sea and its ships were the main focal point of the inhabitants. At Llangrannog, for example, where ninety percent of the male population of the village were sailors at the turn of the twentieth century, *Lloyd's List*, the newspaper which reported shipping movements around the world, would be read on a daily basis by the wives and others in the shed that functioned as the Shipping Office down on the shoreline. These were people whose horizons were global.

By the time of the change from sail to steam in the latter half of the nineteenth and early years of the twentieth century, the great ports of Cardiff, Liverpool, Newcastle, Glasgow, Southampton and Bristol were the main magnets for the sailors of Wales. A large ship sailing from Cardiff might be crewed entirely by men who all originated from the same village in western Wales. The usual practice was for several sailors from the same village to operate as the crew of a ship, commanded by a captain who also came from the same locality. When that particular captain changed his ship, a large proportion of the crew would follow him.

As long as seafaring was important in Welsh coastal communities, the population remained stable. These villages did not experience the depopulation associated with other rural communities during the period up to 1914, because the majority of their sailors were still managing to sustain house and home in the areas in which they were born and bred, although, at any given time, it was mostly the wives who were actually living there.

In fact the switch from sail to steam brought little change to conditions for the sailors. The crew still lived in the fo'csle, and even as late as 1939 open bridges lacking any shelter were the norm. Very often there would be no refrigeration on board, and the crew depended either on salted meat or hard tack as before. A captain from Cardiff, Captain W.B. Thomas, who began his career as an apprentice on one of Evan Thomas Radcliffe's vessels, the *Vera Radcliffe* in 1932, attests to the conditions:

'Our accommodation amidships was divided into a sleeping room and a mess room. We slept in iron bunks upon straw mattresses – donkey's breakfasts and straw filled pillows. Rough, army type blankets covered us during the short spells we were allowed to sleep. In the tropics we slept in hammocks on the poop. The hammocks were used because our accommodation had no cooling system, not even a fan. In any case when in port after 6 p.m. there was no electric power or light as the generator was shut down to save paying the Donkey Man overtime. We then lit up our oil lamps which swung in brass gimbels.

We were paid £40 a year: overtime was often worked but never paid for. We were on a starvation diet and as soon as the contents of the communal ice chest on deck thawed in the tropics our only fresh meat was 'weevil' picked out of our morning 'burgoo' [sort of porridge]. Our staple diet then became salted beef and pork which were quite tasty and a welcome relief from the rotting remains of so called fresh meat which the steward tried to serve us. Coffee, well laced with chicory and sweetened with molasses. Fresh bread served alternatively with hard biscuits. When the butter ran out we were supplied with beef dripping. We were issued with one tin per man per week of condensed milk. Instead of removing the lids we punched two holes in them in a vain bid to keep cockroaches out. As we blew into one hole the milk emerged from the other accompanied by cockroach corpses swollen to bursting point with milk. During 'salt tack days' we collected a mug full of lime juice said to prevent scurvy. Fresh water was drunk twice a day from the gallery pump after the mate had removed the padlock and chain from its handle. I can not say that a few hard times did me any harm.'

Times have changed since then and the sea only attracts a very few from the coastal villages. Within fifty years a way of life has gone and sailors are more scarce than ever. David Loshak, a correspondent in the defunct magazine *Now* reports:

> The bracing sting of salt and spume: the exhilaration of pitting wits against the treacheries of currents, winds and waves. Our latter day Magellans sit remote above the swells, capsuled in double glazed security, cosseted by automatic navigation aids and perhaps misled by them, for they lack the true visual perspective and are deaf to the living sounds of the heaving ocean. It is the atmosphere of boredom, unreality, distorted perception, lack of mental stimulus the worst possible recipe for men to whom life-preserving adrenalin needs to course.

The merchant fleet is now of little significance; the number of vessels flying the red ensign has diminished enormously and the whole fleet now consists of fewer ships than were in Cardiff alone in 1900. At that time, Wales had a large number of shipowners; today there are only two companies in existence, both of which are based in Cardiff, with less than a dozen ships to their name – ships that never visit Wales. For the most part people do not know which international company controls trade to and from Britain, or where the profit from this traffic ends up. Ships flying the flag of Liberia, Honduras, Taiwan and Hong Kong are seen all over the world and the crews can come from several countries, from the Philippines to India, but there are very few from Wales. Once again, as in the Middle Ages, the Welshman is not much of a sailor.

In the past, when trade was flourishing and a large number of ships were at sea, the sailor – perhaps unfairly – was considered to be a somewhat

irresponsible and unruly individual, who took full
advantage of all the various pleasures laid on for him
in the ports of the world.

Certainly, Butetown – or Tiger Bay – in Cardiff was
considered to be equivalent to Scotland Road in
Liverpool and the most dubious areas of ports such as
San Francisco, Buenos Aires and Hamburg. Given the
hardships of life at sea and the length of voyages, it is
little wonder that sailors – including the Welsh – would
avail themselves of the pleasures on offer in the big
ports. In the golden age of seafaring between 1860 and
1946, Cardiff was considered to be an easy port in
which to find a ship because there was so much traffic
there. A large proportion of the ships which came to
Cardiff from Antwerp, Rotterdam or Hamburg would
arrive in ballast, and usually the sailors would be paid
the wages owed to them at the end of the voyage.
Within a mile or so of Cardiff docks, there would be
thousands of thirsty sailors with money to spend. One
observer remarks:

Cardiff is the most undesirable port in the world –
the dumping ground of Europe. On the waterfront a
variety of land sharks, land rats and other vermin
which made the hapless mariner their prey; in the
shape of bar keepers, landlords, clothiers,
prostitutes and boarding house keepers. Land
sharks devoured him limb from limb, while the land
rats constantly nibbled at his purse.

Generally, very few sailors would go much further
than the confines of Butetown. In Tiger Bay there
were over sixty pubs, ranging from respectable
establishments such as the *Big Windsor* and the *Dowlais*,
to the more basic amenities of *The Rothesay Castle
(House of Blazes)* and *The Little Windsor (The Snake Pit)*.
One observer provides this description of *The Rothesay
Castle*:

At the House of Blazes there was a bar on street level and underneath was a dive they called the *Rat Pit*. It was one of those places you could knock at the door at any time and get a drink. Next door was an Arab boarding house. You used to be able to go in there and pay a fixed sum to enter the card game . . . There was a card game going twenty four hours a day, seven days a week.

And then there was the inn, the *Packet*:

It consisted of one large room. In the middle stood two large ladies of indeterminate age. They dressed in black and they organised all the activities of the ladies of the night. It was a dark gloomy cavern and you could hardly see the end of it, it was so dark.

As in modern-day Cardiff Bay, there were plenty of places to eat in Tiger Bay, such as the *Big Windsor* and the *Dominion*, which were renowned for their food. Others, such as the *Star of India*, sold everything but food. One correspondent observes:

Louis Fenwick's *Star of India* was called a café, but it was not, it was a brothel. There used to be an old iron bogie in the middle of the floor, and all the girls would be sitting round it, drinking. If you wanted to take one of the girls you took her upstairs. Café? All they had in the window of the *Star of India* was a couple of jars of old sandwiches. Louis never sold a sandwich in his whole life.

The old Butetown was an extremely dangerous place. If a ship was short of crew, there were the 'Crimps', who were prepared to find crew by collecting drunks, possibly by hitting them on the head and carrying them off to the waiting ships. Many a seamen would wake up to find himself on a strange ship in the middle of the Bay of Biscay on his way to Valparaiso or Fremantle, having had very little time in Cardiff to taste the pleasures of the city.

There was another side to Butetown, of course, as with every harbour town. As well as the hordes of seamen there were shipowners, all sorts of businessmen, butchers such as Messrs. Clode and Patterson, merchants, ship chandlers such as Cravos Frazer and Evan Hughes, and all sorts of industrialists, who manufactured everything from anchors and chains to sails and fuel. There was also every variety of hotel and shop to meet the sailors' needs, the most famous of these being that of George Jones (Jones the Goat), who came originally from Llanddowror in Carmarthenshire and who kept a shop in Bute Street. Jones the Goat was a zealous chapel-goer and an enthusiastic freemason. As well as selling all kinds of merchandise to the sailors – from clothes to shoes, from ropes to crockery – Jones was also very willing to find a crew for any ship's master who needed his help. He would know who was home on leave and ready to return to sea. In fact Jones' information was so thorough that he became known as the *Welsh Consul*. He was also more than willing to act as a moneylender to sailors. When a sailor signed on with a particular ship, he would receive an agreement known as an 'advance note', which undertook to pay the sailor at the end of a voyage. Jones was willing to exchange these agreements for cash, paying seventeen shillings and sixpence in the pound for his services.

The docks at Cardiff have undergone enormous change, and now Tiger Bay and Butetown have become Cardiff Bay – immaculately respectable but devoid of its colourful character of the old days.

Of course other ports had their 'Sailortown' like Cardiff. There was Port Tennant road in Swansea, Dock

Street in Newport and even areas in Pembroke Dock, Caernarfon, Cardigan and Porthmadog, with pubs and clubs, which met the needs of sailors and provided facilities for them to enjoy life on shore.

However, the popular image of the sailors of the past as hard workers returning from long voyages, sampling the dubious delights of the ports of the world, is not always accurate. Sailors were not all 'Jolly Tars', spending their entire wages in just a couple of days' carousing in 'Sailortown'. In sailors' diaries, particularly those from western and northern Wales, there are references to teetotal and God-fearing mariners who would hold an *ysgol gân* [a singing school] on board ship in some far-flung part of the world. Captain Ben Jenkins from Llangrannog, for example, would transfer a small harmonium from ship to ship to accompany the *ysgol gân*, which would be held on a regular basis on board those ships of which he was master. A carpenter from Cardigan on one of Evan Thomas Radcliffe's vessels used to buy a supply of biblical textual expositions for whatever syllabus he was studying in the Sunday School at home, and a Sunday School would be held on board ship every week in exactly the same way as in the Tabernacl in Cardigan. Of the two hundred and forty-one members of Yr Hen Gapel in Aber-porth in 1902, twenty-seven were sea captains and five of the eleven chapel elders were captains.

Another example was Captain Thomas Williams of Newport – the ship's captain who refused to sail on Sundays and who gave each member of his crew a biblical verse to learn every day. On Sundays, they would have to recite them in front of the ship's complement even if the ship was in the middle of the Pacific Ocean.

Life was certainly hard for sailors, and as late as

1939 fatal accidents at sea were three times more common than they were throughout the coal industry in Wales. The quality of the food on some ships remained poor and even in 1958 there was one shipping company from Cardiff which set a daily rate of a shilling and four pence to meet the crew's needs.

Although apprenticeship was common enough on ocean-bound sailing and steamships, only a tiny proportion of seamen who started out as apprentices managed to climb to the highest rung of the profession. The usual career path for a boy who wanted to go to sea was to serve as a deckboy or cabinboy before becoming an ordinary seaman. This was described as 'going before the mast'. After gaining some experience, he could be promoted to 'able seaman'. After four years of service, some sailors might be able to go to college in Cardiff or Liverpool to obtain a second mate's certificate. Then, after further service, they could take a first mate's and master's exam. Apart from officers, ships also carried a number of specialist craftsmen – carpenters, sailmakers and coopers.

Seamen's wages were low. For example, my father (Captain D.J. Jenkins) received a wage of fifteen shillings a month when he went to sea in 1897, a little bit better than his brother (Captain John Jenkins) who went to sea four years earlier for ten shillings a month. Even that was better than the wages received by their uncle (Captain Elias Evans), who went to sea on a New Quay ship for a mere seven shillings and sixpence a month. Elias, it should be said, was only nine years old when he went on his first voyage from Ynys Lochtyn, near Llangrannog, to Lourenco Marques in East Africa.

Until the beginning of the twentieth century, it was not unusual for some of the primary schools on the coast of Wales to teach seamanship as part of the curriculum. Sometimes sailors would also join such classes between voyages. In every town and village of any size on the coast there were schools of seamanship, many of them run by women. At Llangrannog and New Quay, Porthmadog and Caernarfon, strong-minded women would run the schools of seamanship, including such famous instructors as Miss Sarah Jane Rees *(Cranogwen)* and Mrs Ellen Edwards in Caernarfon.

Despite their romantic image, the cargo ships, both sail and steam, were a world apart from the splendour of the ocean liner. The tramp steamer plied a very slow passage round the world; the world, however, depended completely on both them and the men who sailed them.

Although the last sailing ship had departed over the horizon from the small ports and beaches of western and northern Wales long before the turn of the nineteenth century, the practice of going to sea did not disappear. By now, the big ports were the attraction. The steamship owners in the big ports preferred sailors from rural Wales because they knew how to handle a ship in difficult situations on a rugged coastline.

In 1890, on the fifteen ships owned by Evan Thomas, of Aber-porth, and his partner Henry Radcliffe, twelve of the masters were from southern Ceredigion and north Pembrokeshire, and a considerable number of the crews on all their ships were from the same region. Liverpool shipowners who originated from northern Wales likewise employed many of their crews from that area.

Welsh was the first language on board many ships and it is alleged that one or two of the black stokers from Butetown were also Welsh speakers.

Smugglers and Pirates

With so much maritime activity along the Welsh coast, it comes as no surprise that not everyone was as honest as they might have been. For instance, there are references to the way in which the inhabitants of Carmarthen Bay, who were known as 'Gwŷr y Bwyelli Bach' [the hatchet men], would endeavour to lure ships to their doom around Pembrey and Burry Port, by setting false lights on the shore. Once a ship had struck the rocks or had beached on the sand, the cargo would be pillaged. The setting of false lights on the cliffs was also a common practice in the Llantwit Major area and along the cliffs of the Vale of Glamorgan.

During the sixteenth century, the rich merchants of Tenby, and the customs officers and gentry of Pembrokeshire in general were heavily involved in the business of smuggling wine and luxury goods, and were quite prepared to attack shipping. In 1592, for example, pirates from Pembroke attacked four heavily laden ships bound for Cardiff and Bristol. Given the heavy tax on the import of tobacco, silk, brandy, wines and all sorts of luxury goods, smuggling was an extremely lucrative activity. There are caves, often bearing the name *Ogof Tobaco* [tobacco cave], dotted along the Welsh coast, which testifies to how common it was to import contraband throughout the country. For example, when the Reverend Howell Harris came on a visit to the parish of Penbryn where I was born, he railed against those who were 'cheating the king of things excised'. No wonder the valley leading from Llanborth Farm to the sea was called Cwm Lladron [thieves' valley].

Ships from many countries would sail along the coast of Wales and many of them came to grief on her rugged shores, which put a great deal of temptation in the way of the inhabitants. On the 13th of December 1816, for example, a French brig was sheltering near Aber-porth. The anchors failed to hold her and she was wrecked on the rocks of Caerlwyd Beach near Penbryn. She was carrying a cargo of wine and liquor, but within a few hours the entire cargo had been removed to the homes of the local populace. There was binge drinking on a mammoth scale, and several members of Capel Penmorfa were expelled, not to mention the seven individuals who actually died from excess drinking. A contemporary report states that:

> . . . a large body of the neighbouring peasants assembled and pillaged part of the cargo and drank so immoderately that several became the immediate victims of their beastly excess.

The above and other equally inhuman and disgraceful conduct on the part of the people termed 'wreckers' has called forth the laudable interferences of the Bishop of St Davids. We have just met with the following circular . . .

'Revd Sir.

The disgraceful transactions which have lately taken place on the coast of Cardiganshire and Pembrokeshire induce me to request you to write to all the clergy of your Deanery whose parishes lie on the sea coast and to inform them that it is my warmest wish and injunction that they will lose no time in representing to their congregations, in terms sharper than any two edged sword, the cruel and unchristianlike enormity of plundering wrecks; and that for the future that they will preach to them on this subject once a quarter and press strongly on their consciences the flagrant criminality of this inhumain practice and disgraceful to them as Britons and Christians.

The eighteenth century was age of the smuggler. During that century an almost constant state of war existed with France and other countries, which was extremely costly to the British government, and for this reason heavy duties were placed on a large number of commodities – tea and tobacco, all kinds of alcohol, salt and soap, candles and coal – tariffs which people sought to avoid if they could. Circumstances were ideal, therefore, for running contraband to the remote beaches of Wales. Once again, Irish ships carrying goods from the continent were very regular visitors to Cardigan Bay, as were ships from Bristol and Somerset, which also made repeated trips to the beaches of the Vale of Glamorgan and Gwent. As well as these outside operators, Wales had its own smugglers – rogues such as Jack the Bachelor, the leader of a violent gang of mariners from the Sully and Aberddawan area in the Vale of Glamorgan, and Thomas Knight, a shipowner from Barry who was driven out of that town in 1785.

Of course, the Vale of Glamorgan, and Sully Island in particular, has a long association with illegal maritime activities, and at the end of the sixteenth century there were a number of pirates operating in the Bristol Channel. The most famous of these was John Callice from Sully, who also operated in the west, out of the Angle area near Milford Haven. Funded by the gentry, he would usually spend part of the year preying on ships near the Pembrokeshire coast. The pirates of Sully would openly sell their booty on the streets of Cardiff and Swansea.

The perennial activities of pirates from Wales and western England was very lucrative. The mid-eighteenth century was an extremely busy period all along the coasts of western and northern Wales. In 1757, a ship from the New Quay area – the *Swallow*, under the command of David Evan Morris smuggled a cargo of salt, tea and spirits. At that time, the area also had its own infamous smuggler, Siôn Cwilt, who has become part of the folklore of southern Ceredigion. He lived in a small cottage on the moorland between the square at Post Mawr (Synod Inn) and Talgarreg. He earned himself a reputation as a tough, uncompromising individual who was something of a hero among his contemporaries – the moorland east of the main road from Cardigan to Aberaeron has actually become known as Banc Siôn Cwilt.

Some of the smugglers' ships would cover a considerable distance from Anglesey to the Bristol Channel, and would spend time near Bardsey Island, the island of saints, ready to ambush ships laden with cargo on their way from Liverpool. In his small volume *Hen Longau a Llongwyr Cymru* [Old Ships and Seamen of Wales] David Thomas writes:

> There was an armed cutter called the *Fox* smuggling along the coasts of Wales in 1773, in the Bristol Channel, Cardigan Sea and along the shores of Anglesey. The revenue ship caught sight of her one day off Bardsey Island, but because she was a large vessel of some one hundred tons, the captain of the revenue ship – the *Hector* – sailed to Haverfordwest to join up with two other ships – the *Lord Norah* and the *Cardigan* – for support. They heard that the *Fox* was not far from New Quay and they set off in pursuit, but failed to catch her. The customs officer requested more men on board, vowing to catch the *Fox* or die in the attempt . . . In the course of a year, the smugglers had sold at least twenty thousand pounds worth of goods along the coast in the vicinity of New Quay.

Smugglers were equally common in north Wales, and large-scale smuggling took place on the Llŷn

Peninsula and even around Llandudno and Conwy, but the most famous of the pirate gangs operated along the western coast of Anglesey. Remote spots such as Niwbwrch were renowned as landing-places for tobacco, brandy and wine, which was sold to the local inhabitants. This was probably the location for the novel *Madam Wen*, a romantic tale of a female Robin Hood, which was allegedly based on the activities of Margaret Williams of Chwaen Wen, Llantrisant, Anglesey, in the eighteenth century. Creigiau Crigyll near Holyhead was the haunt of the notorious pirate gang 'Lladron Creigiau Crigyll' [the robbers of Creigiau Crigyll], who successfully intercepted heavily laden cargo vessels bound for the Mersey.

One development that made smuggling less profitable was the abolition of duty on salt, which had been such a burden to ordinary people. After its abolition, it was no longer worth buying salt from smugglers. With the removal of their respective duties, the same became true for candles and for fuel. In addition, customs officers were becoming more successful. Finally, in 1786, legislation was passed whereby every ship had to be registered. This involved the naming and registration of every vessel, and the recording of where and by whom it was built, its rig, who and how many people owned it, together with the name of its master. It became much more difficult to hide a ship under some remote cliff, and was now possible to trace every vessel that sailed.

Although more recently smugglers have been viewed as romantic characters, generally speaking they were a cruel and violent bunch, who were prepared to challenge the law of the land and fight tooth-and-nail with the authorities. Their main enemies were the excisemen who were responsible for law and order on the coast.

The Customs Office was established in Britain as long ago as 1643 and duty was levied on beer, wine, spirits, tobacco and other goods as a temporary measure to pay for the Civil War, but in time, all sorts of goods were added to the list of items which were considered suitable for taxation. Rather than being a temporary measure, customs officers are still with us today and are an integral part of the Inland Revenue. The customs service has always been disliked, and easily provokes popular hostility and loathing.

In the early years, the service in Wales had three main offices: at Chepstow, Cardiff and Milford Haven, as well as having an office at Chester which was responsible for northern Wales. Apart from these there were sub-stations for customs at Neath, Swansea, Pembroke, Cardigan, Aberystwyth, Carmarthen, Caernarfon, Beaumaris and Conwy. Customs officers living in many of the coastal villages were non-Welsh speakers, and were hated by most of the local inhabitants. The excisemen were known as 'Riding Officers' and the service in Wales was set up in 1698, when smuggling was spreading rapidly in the country. These officers were each responsible for a designated stretch of coastline. They faced a hectic and challenging time over the next century, and in 1809 it was decided that an additional group known as the Preventative Water Guard would be established. Their job was to guard the coast in small fast boats known as the Revenue Cutters. These officers all came under the supervision of the Inspection Captains.

The usual punishment for smuggling, if it did not result in transportation to Australia, was to spend a period in the Royal Navy. After all, many smugglers were bold and experienced sailors and they were extremely valuable to the navy, which stood in the front line of the fight against the French, or any other enemy.

The recruitment of sufficient seamen was essential, and men were employed to act as members of the Press Gangs which became such a menace to young men in coastal communities. Everyone was at risk – farm labourers and craftsmen might be caught while enjoying a day's leisure in the fair or the market. But the preferred victims were sailors from trading ships, because of their experience. Ships' masters would often pay protection money as a form of insurance against such crude methods of recruitment. The amount that was paid could be as little as half a crown per sailor, to eleven shillings and sixpence for a more experienced mariner.

In the history of unlawful activities at sea, the contribution of the smugglers and pirates of Britain was relatively small compared to the deeds of the pirates of the Caribbean – men such as Harri Morgan from Gwent, and Bartholomew Roberts (Barti Ddu) from Little Newcastle in Pembrokeshire –

'Barti Ddu o Gasnewy' Bach
Y morwr tal â'r chwerthiniad iach
    Efô fydd y llyw
    Ar y llong a'r criw
Barti Ddu o Gasnewy' Bach.'

Barti Ddu from Little Newcastle
the tall sailor with a belly laugh
    he'll command
    the ship and all its crew
Barti Ddu from Casnewy' Bach.

It is very unlikely that this romantic image of the pirate, which derives from the pen of the poet I.D. Hooson, is entirely accurate. Roberts was obviously sufficiently respected and cruel to be chosen from among the rest of the crew to take over as the master of the *Royal Rover* when the captain, Captain Hywel Davies, was killed in a battle in the Caribbean. Roberts was born in 1682 and went to sea at the age of thirteen, serving on naval ships and then for a while on a number of slave ships between western Africa and the Caribbean. Dominating the Caribbean, he was considered to be an audacious and highly skilled mariner, particularly when he managed to capture the *Sagrada Familia* from the middle of a convoy of forty Portuguese warships, which were on station specifically to protect the vessel from the pirates who were rife in that part of the world. It is said that Roberts returned to Britain after a particularly successful voyage in 1721 with eighty million pounds' worth of treasure. In 1722, however, the end came when he was killed near Parrot Island by the crew of *HMS Swallow*, which sailed under Captain Challoner Ogle. Roberts was killed and the crew taken prisoner, and many of them were hanged for their misdemeanours. One historian gives the following description of Barti Ddu:

> Barti was an officer on the pirate ship of Captain Hywel Davies, and on the Captain's death, Barti was chosen to take his place at the age of 37. He is said to have been tall and dark and liked to wear bright clothes. He wore a gold chain around his neck, golden bracelets on his wrists and a yellow cap with a red feather on his head. Barti was a remarkable man in many ways. Despite being a pirate, he was said to be a teetotaller and great respecter of the Sabbath and would hold a religious service for the sailors on board his ship every Sunday. He also took a delight in poetry and music. While his ship was at anchor near Parrot Island he was caught unawares by *HMS Swallow* on the 10th of February 1722 and received a fatal wound to his

neck, and he was thrown into the sea as was the practice in those days. He was forty years old when he died and during his short time as a pirate he captured and defeated over 400 ships.

No wonder the final words of the bravest and most daring of the Caribbean pirates were:

'Bywyd llawen ond un byr' – 'a happy life but a short one'.

The other infamous Welsh pirate, Harri Morgan (c. 1635-1688), was an entirely different character from the down-to-earth Barti Ddu of Little Newcastle. Morgan was of aristocratic stock from the Llanrhymni area in Monmouthshire. He was related to the famous Morgan family of Tredegar. He emigrated to the West Indies and established Port Royal in Jamaica. This port had the reputation of being the roughest in the area, and of being a haven for a large number of pirates. Harri Morgan was the most famous and most violent among them: he attacked Spanish ships in their hundreds and raided the trading centres and magnificent houses of the Spaniards in the Caribbean. He secured thousands of pounds for the British Crown and was knighted and appointed Deputy Governor of Jamaica despite the cruelties he inflicted as a pirate.

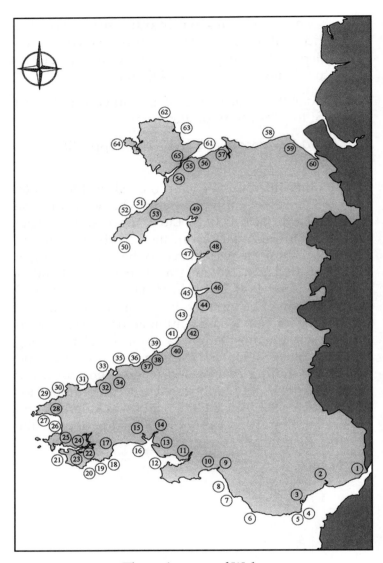

The main ports of Wales

MAP INDEX

PART II – THE PORTS OF WALES

1.   THE BRISTOL CHANNEL

i)   Chepstow

This ancient town on the banks of the Afon Gwy has a long history as a port. Ships would come here during the Middle Ages, bringing essential supplies to the substantial garrison which controlled the border between Wales and England from the impressive fortress overlooking the Afon Gwy. Over the centuries, the Forest of Dean and the counties of Monmouthshire and Gloucester have been one of the most important industrial areas in Britain. Coal and iron were produced here, along with timber products such as charcoal, and oak bark for the leather industry, as well as other types of wood that were in demand. The most important was oak, which was generally used for building warships for the English Navy.

Situated at the mouth of the river, Chepstow was the natural port for exporting forest products. The river was very deep here and the difference between the low and high tide was immense. Apart from its salmon fishing industry, which used flat-bottomed craft anchored midstream and fish traps along its banks, the Afon Gwy was one of the most important of Britain's waterways. The river was navigable as far as Hereford. A large number of important industries were located along its banks, particularly the iron furnaces around Tintern. When the local ore was exhausted, Tintern had to depend on ore imported from Whitehaven in north-west England. The iron was shipped as ingots all over the country. In the early nineteenth century, when there was a tinworks at Llechryd on the Afon Teifi, for example, there was regular traffic between Chepstow and Cardigan. Although there is evidence pointing to Chepstow having been an important port during the Middle Ages, it was in the seventeenth century, with its increase in trade and industry, that it reached its full extent. Chepstow was important enough to be designated a Port of Registry for a large number of vessels, a status it would enjoy up until 1882, when it was replaced by Gloucester.

Apart from its exports and imports, Chepstow was also important as a transfer point where foreign cargoes would be moved on to the trows – relatively small craft which would then sail all the way up the Afon Gwy to Hereford.

Before the railway bridge was built in 1852 and the tunnel under the Severn in 1886, there were ferry services to Bristol and across the Severn, and another from Beachley to Aust. This ran regularly until the 1960s, when it was replaced by the Severn Bridge.

Although Chepstow did not continue as a major port in the same way as Newport and Bristol, it was important as a centre for shipbuilding. Despite a history of large sailing ships being built at Chepstow as far back as the eighteenth century, it became famous after 1874 with the establishment of *Fairfield Shipbuilders* by James Rowe, who was from Devon. Between 1870 and 1914, as many as forty-seven steam ships, some of them as large as 6,600 tons, were built there. In 1915, with the huge demand for ships during the war, three new slips were built to construct a number of vessels for the merchant navy. By 1922 everything had come to an end, with the exception of a short-lived revival during the Second World War, when *Fairfield* produced dozens of Tank Landing Craft, which proved so valuable in the Normandy landings of 1944.

ii)   Newport

The Afon Wysg [River Usk] is said to be the deepest river in Wales and, like the Afon Gwy, Taf and Rhymni, experiences a huge variation between its high and low tide. Newport lies at the mouth of the river, and is still one of the busiest ports in Wales: it exports all sorts of manufactured goods from the eastern valleys of Gwent, and imports a broad range of cargoes, from iron ore (imported up until 2002) to bananas.

Newport is somewhat older than Cardiff, which lies about twelve miles to the west. It was reported in 1877 that:

> For fifty seven days or a sixth of the year on which vessels drawing 20 ft 10 inches of water would have been neaped at Cardiff, they could have left the Alexandra Dock in Newport on the same day.

During the sixteenth century, with such favourable conditions on the Wysg, trade developed a few miles from the mouth of the river at Caerleon, which had been one of the main bases for the Roman legions in Wales. The river was certainly used by the Roman invaders for transportation to and from their spectacular fort at Caerleon. In time, the Usk valley became one of the most important industrial areas in Britain. Surprisingly enough, Newport's prospects were not considered to be particularly favourable at the end of the eighteenth century. A customs officer based in the area in 1775 observed:

> No coal can ever be raised in this part in order to be shipped for exportation or to be carried coastwise; its distance from the water rendering it too expensive for such sales.

Little did he realise that his prophecy for Newport would prove false, and that great things were in store for the mouth of the Usk. In 1797, some twenty years later, as much as 6,939 tons of coal were exported from Newport and from quays along the banks of the Afon Wysg, following the opening of the canal to Crymlyn, Pontnewydd and Pontypool from the heart of the Monmouthshire coalfield. With the opening of the tramway to Cwm Sirhywi in 1805, and another to Basaleg and the Rhymni Valley in 1826, and the *Eastern Valleys Railway* to Blaenafon in 1852, trade was booming in the region. In the years before 1800, a mere sixty-five tons of coal was exported annually from the quays on the river bank; within ten years as much as 500,800 tons of coal and 40,000 tons of iron were being exported. It soon became apparent that the quays on the banks of the Afon Wysg were not suitable for the area's increasing trade. Apart from the coalmines, there were ironworks at places such as Nant-y-glo, Blaenafon and Ebbw Vale, all of which were crying out for improved facilities to export their product. Also of tremendous importance to the region's economy were the tinplate works, the Japan Ware and other industries. Thus, in 1858, the first enclosed dock – the town dock (later known as the North Dock) – was opened in Newport, followed in 1875 by the Alexandra Dock (later known as the South Dock). In that year a total of 943,474 tons of coal was exported and 18,700 tons of iron ore imported. By 1880, a total of 2 million tons of coal was being exported and 481,249 tons of iron ore imported. The export of coal reached its height, in the same way as at Cardiff, with a total of 5.9 million tons that was shipped from the dock in 1913. With three dry docks to handle large ships, Newport is one of the largest ports in Britain, and with the phenomenal development of the Llanwern steel works during the last quarter of the twentieth century there was a correspondingly impressive increase in trade at Newport. The large-scale reduction in the iron and steel industry and the closure of the majority of the Welsh steel works in 2000-2001 meant the end was approaching for much of the activity at Newport.

iii) Cardiff

When one views the splendour of Cardiff's Docklands area today (much of it built in a tasteless style that may be seen anywhere in the world), it is difficult to believe that less than a hundred years ago, Cardiff was one of the most important ports of Britain. Present-day Cardiff Bay has little connection with a description of the area less than a century ago as 'the most undesirable port in the United Kingdom, the dumping ground of Europe'.

The Afon Taf, which was so fundamental to the industrial development of southern Wales, flows to the sea in Cardiff Bay. The whole development of the capital city of Wales is bound up with the unparalleled industrial activity of the Taf Valley and its tributaries. If the valleys of southern Wales had remained unchanged as agricultural areas, it is unlikely that Cardiff would have developed into anything more than a market town similar to Cowbridge or Abergavenny.

Cardiff is fortunate in its location. After leaving its

confluence with the Afon Rhondda at Pontypridd, the Taf flows through the narrow steep-sided Tongwynlais gap. There is scarcely room for a railway, a road and a river at this point, and this bottleneck is a considerable obstacle to traffic. To the south, the valley opens out on to the coastal plain and it is in this broad basin, with the Wenallt and Caerffili Mountain forming a barrier to the north, that the city of Cardiff grew up. Also flowing to the west of Cardiff Bay is the Afon Elai, which meanders gently through the magnificent countryside of the Vale of Glamorgan, with its neat villages and high quality agricultural land, leading to an environment that is very different from that at its source. This is the mining area of Tonyrefail where there were coal beds of the highest quality. To the east of Cardiff Bay, the Rhondda flows into the sea, it too having passed through one of the richest coalfields in eastern Glamorgan and Gwent.

The stage for the drama to be played out at the end of the eighteenth and throughout the nineteenth century, therefore, was the land surrounding the bay, with its three rivers, like veins, flowing to the heart of Glamorgan. It was inevitable that such a sheltered bay, with its natural links extending into one of the great global industrial heartlands, would develop into one of the most important ports in the country, exporting the fantastic riches of the south. In spite of its inherent difficulties, which impeded development, Cardiff certainly did develop – rapidly and on an amazing scale. In fact, Cardiff Bay was quite a difficult place for sailors. There was an enormous difference between high and low water levels, and Cardiff Bay, along with Fundy Bay in Canada, is said to have the greatest tidal variation in the world. For hours on end it is impossible for a ship to get near the shore through the sea of mud that is uncovered for long periods. Despite this, Cardiff was the closest and most convenient place to locate export facilities for the incredible wealth pouring out of the industrial valleys.

At the end of the eighteenth century, Cardiff was not much of a town: it was the market centre for an agricultural area. There were a few houses in the shadow of the castle, and the Taf had fairly abundant stocks of fish, particularly sewin. It was a small port, and access from the sea was difficult in the vicinity of the castle. The street name Stryd y Cei, near the Millenium Stadium today, is a reminder that this was the site of the riverside port. The little ships which ventured along the sinuous, muddy course of the Taf for about a mile from the sea, carried grain, livestock, butter, wool and all sorts of agricultural produce to Bristol and other small ports in Somerset and north Devon. The population of the town at the turn of the eighteenth century was no more than 1,870 inhabitants, and Glamorgan's most important town was Cowbridge. As a harbour too, Cardiff was much less important than Sully, Aberddawan and Barry, and there were few signs of the revolutionary developments that were on the horizon.

The tremendous boom in the iron industry around Merthyr was hampered by its twenty-four mile distance from the sea. The only way in which the product of the furnaces could be brought to the coast and to the market-place was on packhorses, which had to negotiate the difficult paths from Merthyr to the nearest point on the coast – Cardiff. Each horse carried a load of some 130 pounds and very often the horses would be looked after by women and children, who were responsible for driving them from the works to the port. With one person in charge of every three or four packhorses, the situation was impossible, and in 1767, in an attempt to find a solution for an industry that relied entirely on exports, a road was built from Merthyr to Cardiff. Despite the rough nature of this new road, it became possible to carry the product of the iron industry to Cardiff in wagons. Having reached this destination, there were still enormous problems to be faced at the riverside port in Cardiff. Only small ships were able to venture up the river and the tide was only high enough for an hour or two each day.

The ironmasters very quickly realised that neither the cart-track nor the primitive port facilities were going to meet their requirements, and a canal was built from Merthyr to the mouth of the Taf at Cardiff. In 1798, the Glamorganshire Ship Canal was opened, financed by the ironmasters. Moving traffic along the canal was not very easy either, and a total of fifty locks had to be constructed in order to overcome the problem of changing levels along the twenty-four mile waterway. The journey from the works to the all-important port still remained painfully slow. Although quays had been constructed at the head of the canal, it was a tricky place to negotiate. There were still two miles to the low tide mark, and it was only possible to use the sea lock for a few hours each day. Mud and all kinds of muck would cause endless problems, and when the canal was opened to Aberdâr in 1812, the congestion at Cardiff became intolerable. Soon the industrialists from the valleys were complaining bitterly about the unacceptable situation at their main port. There was nothing for it but to attempt to build a new dock near the mouth of the Taf.

By 1820, 50,000 tons of goods were passing through the port of Cardiff, and the total was increasing annually, reaching 350,000 tons in 1839. At the entrance to the canal, conditions had become impossible. The Board of Trade reported:

The largest vessel that could be accommodated was only one of 200 tons burthen. The sill of the sea lock was level with the water at high tide. The level of the highest water on the sill in ordinary spring tides was 18 feet 10 inches. At the flood of low neap tides, only from 6ft to 8ft of water could flow over it. At times therefore many vessels were held up for 6 to 8 days before they could pass in or out of the sea lock. Large three-masted vessels could not enter it at all, and had to be loaded outside by means of lighters, a method which was expensive, both because of the double handling of the cargoer and the deficiency of loading on the mud.

However, salvation was at hand, in the form of the second Marquis of Bute. Although it was only occasionally that the Marquis would visit Cardiff, he owned enormous tracts of land in the valleys and on the coast at Cardiff Bay. In 1828 a report drawn up on the port was, naturally enough, extremely critical of its resources which, to a large extent, were an integral part of the enormous empire of the ironmasters – the Guests and the Crawshays, who had become exceedingly rich through the labour of their workers in the Glamorgan valleys and Gwent.

Without doubt it was the second Marquis of Bute who created the city of Cardiff, paying out a total of £400,000 from his own pocket to build the West Bute Dock to the east of the Afon Taf. In its day, this dock, which extended over some nineteen and a half acres, was the largest in Wales. The new dock was opened in 1839 despite the virulent opposition of the ironmasters, who were perhaps unwilling to see anyone else succeed. The West Bute Dock was hugely successful – too successful perhaps, with the perennial problem of over-use reappearing before very long. In an attempt to cut the Marquis of Bute down to size, the Crawshays and the other ironmasters who owned the old canal decided they needed a railway – the Taff Vale Railway – from the valleys to Cardiff. Lord Bute saw his opportunity and he was determined to be part of the new enterprise, despite strong opposition on the part of the Crawshays. Of course Lord Bute was the owner of the new dock, and everyone who used it had to pay the Bute estate for the right to do so. In 1841 the new railway was opened and the port began to prosper. According to one correspondent, there was 'a General admiration for an immense public work completed for the benefit of mankind'. It seems unlikely that the Marquis of Bute acted primarily out of any great love of mankind. The fact of the matter is that he earned money on every ship which came into the port; he was also collecting substantial rents from the land that was being used to build street after street of houses for the workers. On top of everything else, the Marquis was making a large amount of money from the development of the coalfield deep under the valleys. His incentive was materialistic rather than altruistic.

By 1850, there were 900,000 tons passing through the West Bute Dock annually, and before long the dock was found to be far too small, especially as ships increased in size.

Although the Marquis would only be seen in Wales for a few months of the year, his death in 1848 was a great blow to the townspeople, as he was, quite literally, their lord and their greatest benefactor. As John Davies observes:

> . . . in their momentous changes, the second Marquis of Bute played a significant role. To initiate, to influence or to obstruct change, he built up a structure of power and influence in Glamorgan, in

fulfilment of his concept of the land-owning aristocrat as the natural leader of society.

The third Marquis of Bute showed little interest in his father's ambitions; after all, he was only a year old when his father died. However, friends of the second Marquis, Onesipherous Tyndell Bruce and James McNabb, were prepared to fulfil their obligations and to promote the interests of the infant, while lining their own pockets, and in 1855 the second of Cardiff's docks was opened – the Bute East Dock. By this time, coal was king, and Cardiff was becoming extremely prosperous. The Board of Trade reported:

> Oft times, 200 or 300 vessels were anchored in Penarth Roads, either on steam waiting their turn to come into the dock or hoping for a fair wind to proceed on their outward voyage.

The demand for dock facilities was insatiable: steamships were beginning to replace the old sailing vessels, and before long the Bute East Dock was itself too small to meet the commercial demands, which were still increasing apace. In 1874, another new dock was opened – the Roath Basin – and in 1887 a further huge dock, the Roath, came into operation. In 1907, with the opening of the Queen Alexandra Dock, built by reclaiming some 320 acres of land from the sea, the huge port was complete and at the official opening Edward VII acknowledged: 'In the shipping trade of my Kingdom, Cardiff holds an important place.'

The growth of Cardiff between 1850 and the beginning of the First World War was stupendous, a growth comparable only to that of Chicago. Cardiff was Europe's liveliest town – it was the equivalent of the Klondike or Kuwait during the Victorian Age – and it was to this city that thousands flocked, black and

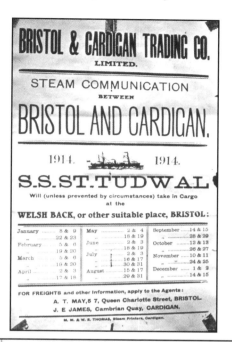

Tenby (Dinbych-y-pysgod), *with fishing boats in the bay. The ketch is one of the famous 'Tenby Luggers', circa 1910.*

Loading slates in Y Felinheli (Port Dinorwig)
(Gwynedd Archives).

Ships of the copper industry in Swansea circa 1905
(Swansea Museum).

*By 1930, tourism had replaced shipping in many parts of Wales,
such as Aberystwyth.*

Barry Docks circa 1908, with the S.S. Italiana
in the graving dock.

Aberystwyth Harbour at the end of the nineteenth century.

Loading coal in Newport (Casnewydd) *Docks.*

Pembroke harbour below the castle circa 1890.

The old harbour of Fishguard (Abergwaun) – *'Y Cwm'.*

*Penarth Docks 1883 (*Welsh Sail, *S. Campbell Jones, 1979).*

Cei Llechi [slate quay], Caernarfon in 2003.

By the quay in New Quay (Ceinewydd).

Fishguard Harbour.

Ships near the lime-kilns on the banks of the Teifi circa 1870. It is likely that the largest of the vessels on the right is the Triton, *famous for carrying immigrants to America.*

A ship from Bristol, loading granite in Porth-gain, Pembroke.

Ships at the mouth of Afon Nyfer in Y Parrog, Newport, Pembrokeshire.

Port Talbot Docks with ships loading coal circa 1930.

Mussel collectors in Conwy circa 1938.

Porth Penrhyn, Bangor 2003.

Porth Penrhyn and the multi seated toilet for the workers, 2003.

Sailmaker – Dafydd Cale – at his work in Bangor around 1975.

Aberdyfi Harbour at its height circa 1890.

Porth Amlwch in its heyday.

*Ships unloading to waiting carts on Traeth y Dyffryn
(Traeth y Llongau) Aber-porth.*

*Alexandra Dock, Cardiff, with a number of ships laid up during a
lean period in the 1930s.*

Aberaeron Harbour circa 1895.

The quay at Aberaeron.

The inner harbour, Aberaeron – Pwll Cam – with ships laid up over the autumn and winter.

Shipbuilding in Cei Bach, 1860 (National Library of Wales).

Porthmadog harbour in its heyday at the beginning of the 20th century (Gwynedd Archives).

Milford Haven (Aberdaugleddau) *Dock with its enormous fishmarket on the quayside.*

white alike, eager to have a stake in its great wealth. For a few years prior to 1914, the port of Cardiff handled more goods than the big ports of Liverpool and London. In 1913 alone, over thirteen million tons of the finest Welsh coal was exported from Cardiff across the world. Cardiff was the global Coal Metropolis. The floodgates of unabated wealth were open and the city attracted businessmen from around the world, all hoping for a share of the spoils.

In Butetown stood the offices of some two hundred shipowners and there were over five hundred ships originating from Cardiff sailing the oceans. It was an incredibly busy and exciting place to be. On a normal day, such as the 1st of June 1904, for example, there were a hundred and fifty ships in Cardiff docks, most of them loading up with coal; there were fifty-eight at Barry and twenty at Penarth. There were a large number of other ships at anchor in the bay, waiting for a berth at the quayside. The scale of the development from a little town around the Norman castle, with a handful of quays on the muddy, meandering river bank, to one of the biggest ports in the world is quite staggering. 'There is no more interesting study in town growth than Cardiff,' a report in 1908 stated:

> At the census of 1851 it was a place of 20,000 inhabitants with no influence and no reputation. Now it is one of the most thriving cities in the country, a centre of trade and commerce. In every respect the development has been remarkable.

However, there were difficult times to come for the city on the banks of the Taf. The global slump in the demand for coal, as it was replaced by fuel oil, meant that the port was in trouble. Cardiff was over-dependent on a single export, and with the terrible problems facing the coalfield and the valleys it was inevitable that the main port would also suffer. In 1964 the last cargo of coal from the Rhondda was shipped from Cardiff, and nowadays there are only two shipping companies left in the city. However, there is a revival on the banks of the Taf today and the hope is that Cardiff, our capital city, will be able to enjoy a very different golden age from the previous one.

iv)   Penarth

Nowadays, the dock at Penarth is a marina for pleasure craft. Today there are luxury flats and select restaurants where coal-loading machinery used to stand on either side of the port. Penarth had one advantage over Cardiff – it was closer to the deep waters of the Bristol Channel. The entire development of Cardiff had been in the hands of the Marquis of Bute, but it was the Windsor Clive family – the owners of St Fagan's Castle – who were the landowners at Penarth. The Taff Vale Railway was responsible for the development of the dock at Penarth and there were good railway connections between the port, which was opened in 1865, and the Glamorgan coalfields. The directors of Cardiff docks were concerned that the Penarth dock, with its railway link to the Rhondda, would replace those at Cardiff, but their fears were unfounded, as the Rhymney Railway, with its links to Monmouthshire, chose Cardiff rather than Newport as the main centre for maritime development.

As the size of ships increased over the years, it was found that Penarth dock was far too small and shallow to give access to the majority of Welsh coal ships. Although the dock remained open until the final quarter of the twentieth century, very few merchant ships still visited the port by that time.

During the golden age of the coal industry, there was a demand for all kinds of landing places to boost coal exports. As well as Penarth, a quay was developed on the mud of the Afon Elai, which could export coal to other parts of Britain without having to pay too much duty.

v)   Barry and the Vale of Glamorgan

By the last quarter of the nineteenth century, the coalowners of Glamorgan were fed up with the overcrowding at Cardiff. Although the docks had been considerably extended since they were first opened, by 1870 it could take several weeks for coal wagons from the Rhondda to reach the docks at Cardiff. These docks were jam-packed, and dozens of ships anchored in Rhodfa'r Barry [Barry roads] awaiting entry. In addition, the Bute family charged a substantial fee for every ton of coal that was exported from the docks. When the Marquis decided to raise the toll of a halfpenny a ton by another halfpenny a ton for the transport of coal wagons at the docks, individuals such as David Davies, Lord Windsor and others decided that they had to break free from the Bute stranglehold and establish a port somewhere else. They looked to a site some seven miles to the west of Cardiff. Although the open beach to the west of Barry Island had been used for centuries, the industrialists of the Victorian Age had to consider a completely new site.

In 1881, Barry was described as an attractive, clean seaside hamlet, with a population of less than a hundred. Despite all the Marquis of Bute's protestations and powerful allies, permission was granted to build a new dock at the mouth of the small river Cadoxton. A company consisting of local landowners, such as Lord Romilly and Lord Windsor, together with coalowners such as David Davies of the *Ocean Coal Company*, who was originally from Llandinam in Montgomeryshire, made a determined effort to create a new dock which would replace Cardiff and the Bute empire. In fact, David Davies went as far as to prophesy that there was no future for Cardiff, and claimed: 'grass will grow in the streets of Cardiff.'

It was a long hard battle and it took two years in the House of Commons to secure permission to build the new docks. There was little love lost between Bute and David Davies and their respective supporters. The matter was debated for eighty-nine days in Parliament before permission was secured, and the new company had to pay £160,000 before the first sod was cut at Barry. In July 1889, the first of the new docks was opened. Accompanying Lord Windsor of St Fagan's, Lord Romilly of Porthceri, R.L.F. Jenner of Gwenfô and Lewis Williams of Cardiff, was the country boy from Llandinam who had reached the top. It is his statue that is seen today overlooking Barry docks, which were indeed his creation.

With a railway network leading to the heart of the Rhondda, Barry grew phenomenally. A second dock was opened in 1898 and by this time the population of the area was thirty thousand. David Davies, Methodist and teetotaller, created Barry in the same way that the Marquis of Bute had created Cardiff years before. The opening of the new docks had a negative impact on Penarth – much more so than on Cardiff, although coal exports from the latter also decreased considerably following development at Barry. However, very quickly, as the south Wales coalfield continued to expand at an enormous pace, there was sufficient demand for the full facilities of all the ports. The following figures show just how important Barry was in the history of the Rhondda coal industry:

1889 – 1 million tons exported
1900 – 7^1/$_2$ million tons exported
1913 – 11^3/$_4$ million tons exported.

It was the success of Barry that forced Bute to re-examine his investment in Cardiff. Although unwilling, he was obliged to invest further and had to pay out £2.25 million to complete the Queen Alexandra Dock.

In its day, Barry was considered to be one of the most modern ports in southern Wales. It had two dry docks where ships were repaired; in its two wet docks there were up to forty-one loading tips for coal, and fifty-six cranes. The dockers of Barry were looked upon as fast-moving and conscientious workers who could load a ship more quickly than anyone else in the docks of southern Wales. Naturally, the town of Barry had its full complement of pubs, eating places and other recreational facilities.

Many of the beaches around Barry had been used in earlier times for the export of farm produce to Devon and Somerset and for the import of all kinds of commodities that would be distributed throughout the Vale of Glamorgan. The most important of these harbours was Aberddawan. Sully Island lay between Cardiff and Barry, and was famous for a very different sort of trade – it was a haven for smugglers and pirates who would harass the ships laden with riches on their way to Bristol from the Caribbean and other parts of the world. As early as the twelfth century Sully Island was a base for ill-doers, the most notorious of whom was the Norman, De Marisco, who was described as 'the Night Hawk of the Bristol Channel'. At a later date, perhaps the most renowned was John Callice in the sixteenth century who is discussed on page 109.

The coast between Barry and Llanilltud Fawr [Llantwit Major] became somewhat notorious, as a result of the activities of the local inhabitants, who would light fires on the high cliffs in order to lure ships to the shore, where they would then loot them.

2.   SWANSEA BAY

i)   Porth-cawl

It is difficult today to imagine Porth-cawl as anything other than a holiday and entertainment resort. A huge funfair and car park now occupy the site of the docks, which at one time were extremely important for the export of coal and iron from the Maesteg and Ton-du area. The Ogwr, Llynfi and Garw valleys were exceptionally rich in coal, iron and other minerals; exporting them from the area, however, presented an enormous problem. Around 1818, an ambitious scheme was being drawn up to build a port at the mouth of the Ogwr [Ogmore], but this site was soon seen to be completely unsuitable. Within a few years, an area known as Pwll Cawl Point was investigated as another possible site. Pwll Cawl Point was different from other harbour locations in southern Wales, insofar as it was not at the mouth of a river that flowed from the heart of Glamorgan and the coalfield. In 1825, the decision was taken to build a tramway

> by Act of Parliament from a place called Dyffryn Llynfi in the parish of Llangynwyd to a bay called Pwll Cawl otherwise Porth Cawl in the parish of Newton-Nottage and to the improving of the bay by the erection of a jetty.

Even Benjamin Disraeli became a shareholder in this enterprise, and by 1828 the work was complete. Unfortunately, sluice gates had not been built for the port, and its early history was somewhat precarious. Out of the horse-drawn tramway, the *Dyffryn Llynvi and Porthcawl Railway Company* came into existence. Although this company experienced a difficult period after its establishment, by 1833 – with the development of the ironworks at Maesteg and Bryn-du, zinc works at Coegnant and several productive coalmines – the facilities at the only exporting port in the area had to be improved. From 1840 onwards a great deal of money was spent on the dock at Porth-cawl.

It is often the case in the history of many Welsh ports that an enterprising individual, or individual family, has been instrumental in their development. In the Porth-cawl area, the pioneers in question were the Brogden family from Manchester. After buying the Ton-du ironworks, John Brogden's company mined coal from several pits in the Ogmore Vale and by 1865 there was a railway running from Nant-y-moel and Ton-du and from Ogmore Vale, which carried huge quantities of coal from the valleys to the sea at Porth-cawl. James Brogden soon realised that the harbour would have to be modernised and extended. Two docks were built near Coney Beach – the outer and inner dock – and in July 1867 the harbour was officially opened when the steamship *John Brogden* sailed in.

Until the end of the nineteenth century Porth-cawl was fairly prosperous, but with competition from Barry in the east and Port Talbot in the west, the port had to close down in 1906 – having enjoyed barely forty years of prosperity.

ii)   Port Talbot

Port Talbot, some six miles from Swansea, is one of the most important locations in Europe for the production of steel, and its huge plants stretch along the shore for several miles to the east of the Afon Afan. Of course before the steel works were built, there were a number of smaller steel and tinplate works in the area. In fact it was these heavy industries that created the town of Port Talbot and led to the expansion of the old villages of Aberafan and Margam.

Since there was plenty of coal around Aberafan, the export trade developed at an early date and, up until the mid-nineteenth century, ships would be tied up at a large number of wharves on both sides of the Afan. In 1834 permission was granted to Emily Charlotte Talbot and *The Company of Copper Miners* in Cwmafan to build a sluice gate across the river, and in 1837 the first dock was opened. With its railway links to the valleys of Llynfi and Garw, the export of coal became important to Port Talbot.

Nowadays there is very little activity in the original dock, but since May 1970 an enormous dock known as the Tidal Harbour has existed, where iron ore is imported to the immense Margam works.

iii)   Neath and Briton Ferry

The Afon Nedd was extremely important in the maritime history of Wales, and the coal, iron and tinplate industries, which were so vital to the area's economy, were dependent to a large extent on the maritime trade. There were ambitious plans to build docks at Neath itself, but these never materialised. Nevertheless, the quays along the banks of the Afon Nedd were extremely busy, despite the fact that ships had to lie on the mud at low water. Although there are not many references to sailing ships being built on the river, there was some activity in the vicinity of Neath Abbey involving the building of steamships, at an early juncture in the history of steam. In 1822, for example, two ships described as Steam Packets – the *Duke of Lancaster* and the *Swansea*, both weighing about 100 tons – were built there. Between 1822 and 1855 twenty-two steam ships – paddle ships and iron tugboats – were built at Neath Abbey.

The banks of the Nedd were the site for a large number of iron and tinworks, and in order to prevent congestion on the river a harbour with docks needed to be built. The docks had two components: the basin and the dock itself. On the shores of the dock, there were at least nine iron and tinworks. In 1938, for example, the following firms were to be found on the dockside:

Briton Ferry Iron Works
Villiers Tinplate Works
Albion Steelworks
Wern Tinplate Works
Whitford Steel Sheet and Galvanizing Works
Gwalia Tinplate Works
Briton Ferry Steelworks
Baglan Bay Tinplate Works
Vernon Tinplate Work

Nowadays, although there are still important industries at Briton Ferry, the port which was at one time so busy is at a standstill. When the sluice gates were removed in around 1970 there was no future for the port, which is now choked with mud, and the ships coming up the Nedd are few and far between. Up until the end of the last century there was regular traffic – including many boats from Europe – carrying coal to a wharf known as the Giant's Causeway. It is strange to think of coal now being imported into the heart of the Glamorgan coalfield. For some years after the Second World War, the Giant's Causeway was used to break up ships, the iron and steel of which was then recycled.

iv)   Swansea

On his journey through Britain, Daniel Defoe talks about Swansea as

> a very considerable town for trade and a good harbour. Here is also a great trade for coals and culm while they export to all the ports of Somerset, Devon and Cornwall and also to Ireland itself, so that one sees a hundred sail of ships at a time loading coal here.

Long before any dock was built at the mouth of the Afon Tawe, the sheltered beaches of Swansea Bay were extremely busy. The town had an advantage insofar as the Tawe valley and its environs were dotted with coalmines as close as three miles or so from the coast, and by the early eighteenth century, coal ships would sail on a regular basis from Swansea to all parts of the west coast of Britain, and to Ireland, France, the Channel Islands, Spain and Portugal.

Since the Swansea area possessed sufficient coal to fire furnaces, the most important industry established in this region and at Neath was the copper industry. Copper had to be imported – initially from Cornwall, and then from Parys Mountain in Anglesey, and later on from Chile. By the end of the nineteenth century, it is said that ninety percent of the copper produced in Britain came from the Swansea and the Neath region. Seventy-five percent of Welsh tinplate was produced within some fifteen miles of Swansea. With the tremendous growth in these industries, a suitable port had to be provided for all the exports and imports associated with a town that was a world leader in the manufacture of metals. Although small ships of up to 60 tons were able to sail up the Tawe for some two miles to the Glan-dŵr area, the situation in Swansea

Bay was inadequate. While Llanelli got its dock in 1828, Cardiff in 1839 and Newport in 1844, Swansea ships were obliged to lie on the estuary mud near one of the quays, or out in the bay itself, for a while longer. In 1827, Thomas Telford, the famous engineer, informed the trustees of the harbour:

> The harbour of Swansea is in my opinion singularly well situated for being rendered capacious, convenient and safe: but that this can only be effectually accomplished by converting both the river and the harbour into floats, totally independent of each other and yet so as to be occasionally connected.

Following years of argument, the first dock was opened on New Year's Day in 1852. This was the North Dock (the site of a supermarket today), and after further years of quarrelling among the trustees, a second dock was acquired – the South Dock (the site of the present-day marina) – in 1859.

As local industry continued to boom, so too did maritime traffic, and before long it became apparent that the two docks to the west were insufficient, and a decision was made to build extensive docks to the east of the Tawe. In 1881 the Prince of Wales Dock was completed; the King Edward VII dock was opened in 1909, and the Queen's Dock in 1920 – the latter being an oil terminal associated with the BP petroleum works at Llandarcy near Neath. With all the traffic from the metal and anthracite industries, from fishing and from a host of other enterprises, Swansea was one of the most important ports in the country. W.J. Jones observed in 1922:

> Thanks to the growth of the copper smelting, zinc spelter, steel, iron, tinplate and other works, there

was probably no other harbour in the kingdom worked by docks where such an amount of traffic was carried on a given water space as in Swansea.

Although there was a certain amount of wooden shipbuilding along the banks of the Tawe, the port did not become a major centre for that industry. The Swansea shipowners preferred investing in cheap ships from Prince Edward Island in Canada. Such ships were built of softwoods rather than Welsh oak. In Canada, William Richards from Swansea built ships by the hundred with his in-laws, the Yeos, while his brother Thomas Picton Richards acted as his agent, and things were very prosperous for them.

In 1876-7, of the two hundred and sixty-three ships listed as being from Swansea, one hundred and twelve of them had been built in Prince Edward Island; thirty-seven came from north-eastern England; thirty-four from the north of Devon; fourteen from Glasgow and only eleven from Swansea. These were slow vessels, designed to carry heavy cargoes of coal and copper – slow ships that ploughed their way around the world through the roughest of seas. In comparison to the shipowners of Cardiff, the Swansea owners stuck with sailing ships, as they had neither the need nor incentive to invest in iron steamships. They were dependent to a great extent on sailors from western Wales to sail their ships: individuals such as Captain William Williams of Llandudoch, who went to sea at the age of thirteen on a local smack – the *Hopewell* – in 1869. By 1875 he and a number of his contemporaries had joined the *Lord Clyde*, one of Tullocks' ships at Swansea, a vessel which was heavily involved in the copper trade.

Between 1877 and 1900 some thirty-two shipping companies were established in Swansea; companies such as *Richards, Burgess and Shaddick, Richard Tullock,* and *Henry Hoskin*. From around 1880 onwards the copper trade began to wane, although sailing ships would still be seen until 1914. The owners of the copper barques were considered a ruthless and uncaring bunch who were prepared to sacrifice others in order to make a profit. Selecting from among the two hundred ships lost in the last quarter of the nineteenth century, Aled Eames records the voyage of one of Henry Hoskin's vessels from Swansea. Hoskin came from Cornwall and he tried to replace the traditional square-riggers with big schooners. One of these ships was the *Bride*:

In May 1882 the *Bride* from Swansea, on her way to Valparaiso, was in great difficulties in a raging force 10 south-westerly close to the Horn. The rigging of her foremast was torn by the winds and the mast itself crashed onto the deck. In such tempestuous seas, the task of shifting the debris after such a disastrous series of events was daunting to say the least. Worse was to follow, however – the mainmast also lost its rigging and some of the surrounding planking was loosened, which allowed a lot of water to get in under the deck. Then the pumps became clogged. With the main mast swaying dizzily and the ship sinking deeper in the stormy ocean, more and more water was forced below decks, until the pumps finally failed. The sea poured into the hold, which contained some 800 tons of Welsh coal. No wonder the captain and crew took to the lifeboats. What is remarkable is that they all survived to tell the tale.

Nowadays, trade at the Swansea port is nothing compared to how it was half a century ago. The fishing industry has long since died out; neither coal nor tinplate is exported, and the closure of the BP works in

Llandarcy means that oil is no longer imported and exported. The ferry service still runs regularly to Cork and has done so since 1987. Museums, pleasure craft, restaurants and penthouse flats now proliferate along the edge of the South Dock and there are plans to extend these facilities to the east of the Tawe, whose waters are now controlled by a dam.

3. CARMARTHEN BAY

i) Llanelli

During the nineteenth century – particularly the last quarter of that century – it could be argued that Llanelli was one of the most important industrial towns in Wales. Although there were numerous coalmines and a major copper works in the Llanelli area, it was to the tinplate industry that the town owed its prosperity. No wonder Llanelli gained its reputation as 'Tre'r Sosban' – 'saucepan town'. By the end of the nineteenth century, Llanelli could be described as a one-industry town. Although that industry had in fact been established as early as 1737 in Cydweli, during the latter half of the nineteenth century it reached its full capacity, with as many as nineteen tinplate works operating in the area, employing the vast majority of the town's male population. It was a gruelling and back-breaking industry.

The growth of the tinplate industry was responsible for the development of the port at Llanelli. The import of iron ore, much of it from ports such as Millom and Whitehaven in north-west England, and the export of manufactured goods required ships. There were limitations to the size of vessel which could negotiate the meandering channels into Llanelli, and since the greatest demand for tinplate was from the USA – Chicago in particular – to make tin cans for meat and other foodstuffs, the cargoes had to be transferred from the small ships of Llanelli to the larger vessels from Liverpool and, to a lesser extent, Bristol. Some firms from the USA invested in tinplate works in the area – for example, *Phelps, James & Co* of New York, who were agents for the export of Llanelli tinplate. This was the firm who, with capital of £50,000, established the *Llangennech Tinplate Co. Ltd* in 1867.

In the 1860s, the tinplate export market was in the hands of local firms such as the *Llanelly Steam Navigation Company* (1862) and the *Llanelly and Liverpool Steam Navigation Company* (1876).

Three or four steamships would sail each week from Liverpool Wharf near the Neville dock to the port of Liverpool. Of course, the main shareholders of Llanelli ships were the owners of the tinplate works, individuals such as Henry Rees and Thomas Stone from the *Burry Port Tinplate Works* and David Samuel of the *Ashburnham Tinplate Company*.

Despite all this activity in 'Tinopolis' over more than a century, the industry's demise was inevitable, and in February 1951 the docks were closed completely. In its heyday, the town had several docks: Pemberton's Dock (around 1805); Carmarthenshire Dock (around 1801); Copperworks Dock (1806; refurbished with sluice gates in 1825), and the North Dock, built in 1903. Despite all the difficulties – as J.K. Brunel observed in 1857, 'Nature has not done much to fit Llanelli for a port' – there had nevertheless been prosperous times.

ii)   Pembrey and Burry Port

What is perhaps most surprising about this stretch of coast is that any sort of port at all was established in the north of Carmarthen Bay, since this area is characterised by dangerous sandbanks that are constantly shifting. The beaches might be suitable for the cocklers of Llan-saint but attempting to keep any sort of harbour open involved a continuous struggle against the elements. Somewhere had to be found to export coal from the Gwendraeth valley, which was considered to be of very high quality. This anthracite, ground and mixed with clay to form *cwlwm*, was one of the main sources of fuel for extensive areas of Pembrokeshire and Ceredigion. Traditionally, three types of *cwlwm* were used – *Cwlwm Hook* from a village on the banks of the Afon Cleddau in Pembrokeshire; *Cwlwm Abertawe*, and *Cwlwm Pen-bre*. Ships would come from New Quay and Cardigan, Llangrannog and Aber-porth to a small harbour built in 1810, to collect many cargoes of *cwlwm*, which was sold to the inhabitants in the west. By 1832, the port of Burry Port had been opened and by the mid-nineteenth century this port, together with Pembrey, controlled the entire wealth of the Gwendraeth Valley coalfield. With the opening of the *Burry Port and Gwendraeth Valley Railway*, both these communities flourished. Major industries were established in the area – from tinplate to copper – and with the unceasing demand for coal export facilities, the dock at Burry Port had to be expanded in 1888. Unfortunately, because of the shifting sands in the bay, the river ports of the Gwendraeth valley were not developed properly and with the increase in the size of ships, there was not much of a future for Burry Port or, indeed, for neighbouring Llanelli.

The history of the Pembrey and Burry Port area contains many disturbing tales of wrecking. Over the course of several centuries, the inhabitants were renowned for luring ships onto the beach at Cefn Sidan in order to plunder their cargoes. No wonder they were know as Pobl y Bwyelli Bach – the Hatchet People.

iii)   Cydweli

As is the case with many of the castle towns of Wales, Cydweli has a long history as a port, and as early as 1229 there are records of King Henry III granting the right to

'Robert de Cadwely', *Magister Navis* [shipmaster], to trade with Gascony in France. This trade involved carrying wool and animal skins to Gascony, and returning to Cydweli with wine and oil. By the early sixteenth century, there was a fair bit of trade between Cydweli and France and Ireland, consisting of the export of wheat, barley, salt fish and beer.

Unfortunately, as is the case in several parts of Carmarthen Bay, the estuary of the Afon Gwendraeth was choked with mud, and the ships were only occasionally able to reach the town of Cydweli. With shifting sandbanks in the vicinity, such as at Cefn Sidan, shipwrecks were frequent. Following the discovery of an extremely rich anthracite coalfield in the Gwendraeth valley, an attempt was made by Thomas Kymer, an industrialist from Pembrokeshire, to improve the harbour. In 1766 a canal was built to the new port in Cydweli. However, because of its inherent difficulties, Cydweli did not do particularly well as a port. For a few years there was a shipbuilding industry there, but before too long the mud and sand became too much, and a local historian observed in 1907: 'the quantity of coal exported from Kidwelly now is insignificant as most of it is taken to Burry Port and Swansea for shipment.'

By 1930 the port of Cydweli had ceased to exist.

iv)   Carmarthen

The Afon Tywi follows a difficult, meandering course from the ancient town of Carmarthen to the mouth of the river at Glan-y-fferi. Nevertheless, despite all obstacles the river has a long history as one of the busiest in south-west Wales, and Carmarthen itself enjoyed its own particular commercial activity which had links to all parts of the world. As far back as the Roman period, Carmarthen – *Moridunum* [sea fort] – imported wine, crockery, oil and jewellery from the Mediterranean, to meet the needs of this populous Roman fort. After the building of the Norman castle on the banks of the river, the inhabitants came to depend on the goods that were brought in by sea, and trade developed enormously during the centuries that followed. There was a regular link with the ports of western England – Bristol in particular, but also Barnstable and Bideford. In addition to the important trade in wool and agricultural produce during the Middle Ages, a close relationship was built up with France, especially with the port of La Rochelle. Although the majority of ships which came to Carmarthen were from France, by the sixteenth century more and more local ships were using the port.

In around 1566, Dr Moelwyn Williams noted that there was a total of six ships owned by Carmarthen merchants:

i) *The Nyghtyngale*: 50 tons. Owners: Richard Lewis Hopkyn and David Ieuan. Crew of ten and two boys. Sailing mostly to Bristol and France.

ii) *Angell*: barque, 28 tons. Owners: Gr Pontin, Morris Hancok and Morris Thomas. Crew of five. Trading with Bristol.

iii) *Mathew*: barque, 18 tons. Owner: Richard Lewys Hopkyn. Crew of five. Trading with Bristol.

iv) *Nycholas*: smack, 8 tons. Owner: Richard Lewys Hopkyn. Crew of three. Trading with Bristol.

v) *Mary David*: smack, 8 tons. Owners: Richard
Lewis and Nicholas Roche. Crew of three.
Trading with Bristol.

vi) *Trynytie Burley*: smack, 8 tons. Owners:
William Burley and John Phylip. Crew of two.
Trading with Bristol.

One ship – the 18-ton *Mychaell* – is recorded as being
owned by John Palmer and David Allan from
Laugharne. This ship traded with western England
with a crew of five. There were very few local ships in
Carmarthen Bay during the sixteenth century apart
from at Carmarthen and Burry Port. At Burry Port
there was one small ship, the 8-ton *Jesus* owned by
Owen ap Jenkyn with a crew of three, which would
trade between Laugharne and Barnstable.

One of the great advantages of Carmarthen was that
it was quite far from the sea, and was thus safer from
attack by the smugglers and pirates who prevailed for
several centuries in Carmarthen Bay. Dr Pococlle noted
in 1751:

There is a good quay to which ships of 150 tons can
come up as they have eleven feet of water. They
have a great trade in butter to London and of wheat,
barley and beans to all parts, mainly coastwise and
they are famous for pickled salmon.

Despite the difficulties the town's mariners faced in
reaching the sea, due to the river frequently changing
its course, Carmarthen was nevertheless a significant
port. In 1831, for example, the local historians Joyce
and Victor Lodwick noted that Carmarthen had fifty-
one ships registered by the port authorities. A total of
four hundred and twenty coastal vessels visited the
port. In addition, there were thirteen ships from
overseas among them, including vessels involved with

the fishing industry in Newfoundland and Nova Scotia. There was also a certain amount of emigration, although this was not always a particularly successful trade. In 1795, for example, a group from Montgomeryshire was reported to have left for Bristol and from there for America on board a ship called the *Maria*. Unfortunately for them, the master of the *Maria* refused to venture up the Afon Tywi [River Towy], and these unfortunates from Powys had to walk all the way to Bristol to board their ship.

Despite these problems, Carmarthen prospered. After all, since 1547, the mayor of Carmarthen had used the title *'Admiral of the River Towy from the bridge at Carmarthen to the bar of the said river'*.

In addition to trade, the construction of sailing ships was also an industry on the river. Between 1805 and 1850, a number of brigs of up to 200 tons and more were launched at Carmarthen. The most significant of these were: the *Mary Anne* (1805); the *Priscilla* (1806); the *Albion* (1813); the *Hero* (1814); the *Margaret* (1834); the *Naiad* (1838), and the *Princess Royal* (1841).

Among the smaller ships built at Carmarthen were the *Carmarthen Packet* and the *Bristol Packet*, but by the 1860s the shipbuilding industry at Carmarthen had come to an end.

In 1830, a steamship service began between Carmarthen and Bristol, but despite confidence in its success, it failed. The *Frolic* came to Carmarthen for the first time in November 1830, but by 1831 it was wrecked in a March storm on Pwynt Nash near Porth-cawl, with the loss of a large number of the crew and passengers. Nevertheless, the merchants of Carmarthen remained hopeful, and another paddleboat was acquired – the *County of Pembroke* – which ran on a regular basis from the quay in Carmarthen to Bristol.

The 1820s were the golden age for the port, despite the vagaries of the river channels, which were often blocked by mud. In 1847 the *Bodallog*, one of the Aberystwyth ships, sank with a cargo of grain at the mouth of the river, and became a danger to shipping for years to come.

During the last quarter of the nineteenth century there was a regular service between Bristol and Carmarthen, maintained by the steamships *Cambria* and *Neath Abbey*, and to Liverpool with the *Ibis* and *Lady Kate*. However, with the advent of the railway in 1852 and the extension of the railway to Llandeilo, Whitland and Llandysul, the demise of the port was inevitable. By 1938, the maritime trade from Carmarthen had come to an end and the port of one of the most important medieval towns was finished.

v)   St Clears and Laugharne

The Afon Taf flows a short distance from its source in the Preseli Mountains, near Pentregalar, to the sea in Carmarthen Bay, near the ancient town of Laugharne. Despite its comparatively small size, this valley has played an important part in Welsh history. This was the site of the court of Hywel Dda, and Gruffydd Jones, the father of Welsh literacy, was rector for many years at Llanddowror. It was also home to the poet Dylan Thomas.

Apart from its literary and cultural links, the Taf valley was also the site of important industries. Llanfyrnach, for example, was the location of the most significant lead and silver mines in southern Wales; its ore was exported from the port of St Clears, about a mile from Laugharne and the mouth of the river. Towards the end of the eighteenth century, the owner of the lead works at Llanfyrnach had ambitious plans to deepen the river between Laugharne and St Clears, so that larger ships could sail all the way up to Llanfyrnach. In 1764 it was noted that: 'Taking the whole together, it is very plain that the adventurers can not lose by this field if well managed.'

With the development of huge quarries at Glôg in the nineteenth century, the Taf valley became extremely important as an industrial centre, and the port of St Clears reflected the activity in the valley. The small town stands a good mile from the mouth of the river and became a port of some significance. In the early nineteenth century an observer noted:

> The town is always busy either with the exports of corn and general produce or with imports of coal, limestone and simple groceries and draperies.

Despite the meandering nature of the Afon Taf, ships continued to sail into St Clears up until the 1850s, when the railway arrived in the area from the south.

Things were somewhat different in Laugharne near the mouth of the Taf. The railway did not reach this ancient town, and for this reason Laugharne continued as a port until the First World War. Of course, as the site of a Norman castle whose garrison depended on maritime transport, the tradition of seamanship in the town was very old. When the town was built in the shadow of the castle, the river was the focus of Laugharne life, and to this day, the mayor is still referred to as a Port Reeve.

For centuries, the wealth and prosperity of Laugharne was based on maritime trade and on the small port which had been established below the castle walls. During the sixteenth and seventeenth centuries, for example, there were a number of shipowners and wealthy merchants living in the town. Not only did

Laugharne have its own ships, but ships would also visit from the rest of Britain and Ireland and elsewhere. Perhaps the most regular of these visitors were ships from France, which brought wines to the borough. Unfortunately, this estuary also silted up rapidly and posed problems for maritime traffic. It was a constant struggle to try to keep the mud at bay, but in the end several of the wharves became choked. Shipowners, such as the brothers Henry and John Butler, attempted to use flat-bottomed boats to overcome the problem. Nowadays, there is not much to show for the activity there once was, because the mud has almost completely covered the old Norman port.

4.   PEMBROKESHIRE

i)   Saundersfoot

When the coal industry in Pembrokeshire was at its height, producing top quality anthracite, the main harbour for its export was the village of Saundersfoot, whose coal trade continued up until the 1950s. The crushing process to make *cwlwm* also took place not too far from the shore. The coal of southern Pembrokeshire was of such high quality that it was rated the best available by the Guinness brewery in Dublin. For this reason, ships from Dublin were regular visitors to Saundersfoot, as were producers of brewing malt from Kent and East Anglia, all of them calling regularly for coal from pits such as Stepaside, Bonville's Court, Reynalton and Grove, which they considered to be the best for the tricky job of heating malthouses.

This coalfield has a long history stretching back to the Middle Ages, when coal was exported from open beaches in the area. From 1806 onwards, a network of tramways was built from the coalmines to the coast, and in 1829 a new port was built at Saundersfoot. An account from 1856 describes a:

> small but strong harbour built of solid masonry. Several schooners were lying in it and an air of bustle and trade prevailed – tramroads lead to the harbour by which the culm and anthracite are brought down, whence they are emptied into the vessels alongside the wharves through large wooden shutes.

Nowadays, the harbour caters for pleasure craft and two or three fishing boats, the area's collieries have become caravan sites, and there is nothing to show that this attractive village was once a major outlet for the export of anthracite.

ii)   Tenby

Today, Tenby is a leading tourist centre in Wales, attracting thousands of visitors who come to enjoy its golden sands, spectacular coastline and a variety of other attractions and entertainment. One of the town's most renowned artists, Charles Norris, observed in 1812:

> Few places can be more productive of gratification than a happy assemblage which artists can seldom discover in any one spot.

From the end of the eighteenth century, the town started to become more popular and, under the influence of Sir William Paxton, saw the development of fashionable houses, the Assembly Rooms, hotels and swimming pools. With the arrival of the railway in 1863, such developments rapidly gathered momentum, attracting thousands of visitors from all over the country, particularly from industrialised areas of southern Wales, visitors who were now within easy and rapid reach of the town.

However, Tenby has a long and venerable history as one of the most important ports of Wales in the Middle Ages. With a Norman castle situated above its natural harbour, Tenby developed a regular trade with France. In 1328 a wharf was built which was to become particularly important for importing French wine and for exporting anthracite to France, Spain and Portugal. Mariners from southern Pembrokeshire were adventurous enough to sail considerable distances from home, and it is not surprising that Saint Julian's church was built on the quayside to enable them to hold prayer meetings before embarking on their voyages – voyages that were undertaken in tiny, fragile craft, able to carry not much more than some ten tons of cargo each. With wine and oil from France, salt from the Oporto region of Portugal, fruit from Spain and agricultural produce from Ireland, the import trade at Tenby was brisk. In addition to the anthracite and *cwlwm* of the area, a variety of flannel cloth was produced by the weavers of Pembrokeshire, as this county was the principal centre of the wool trade in the Middle Ages.

A charter having been bestowed on the town in the fifteenth century, Tenby was an exceptionally wealthy place by the Tudor Age. Municipal power was in the hands of merchants who acquired enormous wealth – wealth that was reflected in some of the houses that can be seen near the harbour. However, their wealth was not always acquired by honest means: they were heavily involved in piracy and contraband, and were willing to import goods from Spain at a time when Spain and England were at war.

The port continued to prosper until the end of the eighteenth century, and in 1724 Daniel Defoe describes the town as having:

> a very good road for shipping and well frequented. Here is a great fishery for herring in its season, a great colliery, or rather export of coals and they drive a very considerable trade with Ireland.

With the disappearance of a large number of local collieries by the end of the eighteenth century, the export trade for coal declined at Tenby. Although the fishing industry continued almost until the beginning of the twentieth century, the harbour developed primarily as a recreational facility. Coal dust and the stink of fish were hardly suitable for a tasteful seaside resort, and the export of coal and *cwlwm* became concentrated in the neighbouring village of Saundersfoot.

To the west of Tenby are a number of beaches such as Manorbier, Lydstep and Stackpole. In 1566, the latter was described as being one of Pembrokeshire's most important harbours. The port continued to transport lime to other parts of Wales up until the end of the nineteenth century, as did nearby Lydstep. The coast from Tenby to Sant Govan's cove is renowned as a landing place for contraband and Ogof Lladron [Robbers' Cave] may still be seen at Lydstep.

iii)   Milford Haven and Neyland

The estuary of the two Cleddau rivers stretches for some ten miles into the heart of southern Pembrokeshire. This was the site of important fisheries, collieries that produced high quality anthracite, and much other industrial activity. Although there were numerous wharves along the banks of the estuary, such as those at Hook, Lawrenny, Burton, Angle, Dale and Cresswell, some of which were associated with the export of coal, Milford Haven was without doubt the most ambitious of these harbours.

To Lord Nelson, who visited Milford Haven in 1802, this unremarkable little port in Pembrokeshire and that of Trincomalee in Sri Lanka were the two best natural ports in the world. Nelson was accompanied on his visit to Pembrokeshire by the founder of the town, Sir William Hamilton, and his young wife. He spoke at the New Inn, which, as a mark of respect, was renamed the *Lord Nelson Hotel*.

As late as 1946, Milford Haven was referred to as 'The best and most foolishly neglected harbour in Europe.' According to an Admiralty handbook:

[Milford Haven] offers the only perfect and accessible shelter from all winds at all times and for all classes of vessels between Falmouth and Holyhead.

Throughout the history of the estuary since the establishment of the new town at Milford Haven in the late eighteenth century, it was dogged by failure: failure to take advantage of the natural resources of a perfect harbour. Of course, over the centuries, there was a history of conquest and immigration, and of ambitious projects that could have led to spectacular success, but a combination of bad luck and failure seem to have prevailed.

There are references to Milford Haven from the ninth century up until 1100 as the centre from which the Vikings would launch attacks on other parts of western Britain. It was here in 878 AD that as many as twenty-three Norwegian ships spent the winter on the Afon Cleddau, from where they raided the coast of Devon. Viking elements are still in evidence in place-names with Scandinavian roots, such as Skockholm, Skomer, Hubberston and Haverford.

Although things were fairly uneventful on the Afon Cleddau after the departure of the Vikings – other than Henry Tudor's landing in Dale on his way to the Battle of Bosworth – the area became a notorious centre for piracy and smuggling. After all, Bartholomew Roberts – Barti Ddu, the pirate king – was a native of Little Newport, not so far from the Cleddau valley. In creeks the whole length of the estuary, all kinds of illegal cargo was landed, and every social class, from the squire in his mansion to the fisherman in his cottage at the water's edge, would delight in the activities of the pirate and the smuggler. One of the leaders in this trade was George Clerk, a customs officer from Milford

Haven, who kept an inn in the village of Angle. Despite his offices as an excise man, he was heavily involved in trading goods to Spain, the number one enemy of the British government during the sixteenth century. He would make other pirates welcome for weeks if not months in the estuary. Angle was the centre for the main perpetrators of this trade – perpetrators such as Fytiplace, John Callice from Sully, and Robert Hicks of Saltash, who made a livelihood from preying on ships in the Irish Sea.

Until the end of the eighteenth century, Milford Haven was a small, insignificant village. Most of its inhabitants were fishermen who became skilled in building boats by the estuary. However, it was not a particularly prosperous place until Sir William Hamilton, who married a local girl, saw the enormous potential offered by the estuary. He decided to establish a new town on its northern shore, and appointed his nephew, Charles Francis Greville, as his agent. In 1790, work was begun on the construction of a new town, and in its wake came a number of important economic developments. The Navy was persuaded to establish a shipbuilding yard for warships in the new town, and Quaker families from Nantucket Island in the United States were persuaded to migrate to Milford Haven to pursue their occupation as whalers. This was a somewhat surprising development, as the South Seas – where the whales were usually to be found – was an enormous distance from Milford Haven. No wonder the fishermen decided to return to Nantucket in 1810, and no wonder either that the Navy decided to move its shipyard to Pembroke Dock on the southern side of the estuary. This was one of the first failures in the ambitious scheme to establish a world-class port and industrial centre in southern Pembrokeshire. For years following the end of the Napoleonic Wars in 1815,

Milford Haven was not particularly prosperous. There was, however, a small amount of shipbuilding, and passenger ships would set out on a daily basis for Waterford and Dublin.

However, the community leaders of Milford Haven were unhappy about the town's status as a rather insignificant port on the shores of the estuary; they dreamt of building a port that could compare in importance to Liverpool and Southampton as a passenger terminal for north America or Australia. Sir William Hamilton's ambitious dream lived on for forty years after his death. In 1845, hopes were high in the wake of plans to build the *Manchester and Milford Railway*, which was meant to ensure a golden age for Milford Haven as a transatlantic passenger terminal. Unfortunately, the railway was never completed, and it got no further than the Llanidloes area. Meanwhile, another scheme was in the offing to build a railway for southern Wales – *The South Wales Railway* – from London and Gloucester to Milford Haven. Unfortunately it was Fishguard rather than Milford Haven that was chosen as the main terminal for the railway. Even worse, despite all attempts to persuade him otherwise, Isambard Kingdom Brunel decided to create a 'new railway town' at Neyland, some five miles from Milford Haven.

By 1856 Milford Haven had lost the battle, and the passenger service for Waterford and Cork now sailed on a daily basis from Neyland. To add insult to injury, the new port and town of Neyland was called 'New Milford'. To this day, there is little love lost between the inhabitants of these two towns on the banks of the Cleddau.

However, despite failing to persuade the authorities to create a first class port at Milford Haven, the grand dream had not entirely died, and in 1874 the *Milford*

Docks Company was established with the purpose of creating a transatlantic port. By 1888, the new dock was complete. A local paper in 1882 observed:

> The natural advantages of Milford Haven are very great and with the improvement in docks, railway and pier it will inevitably become a formidable rival to Liverpool.

Unfortunately, once again, the dream was not realised. Although the *City of Rome* called there once on its voyage from Liverpool to New York and the *Gaspesia* on her way to Canada, no regular service was ever established, and by 1900 that particular dream was over.

Subsequently another possibility presented itself – the sea-fishing industry. The dock owners were certainly not too keen to see this particular development, which they felt to be rather degrading. As the local paper commented:

> The Docks Company have not built their great docks to attract fishing smacks but they will not look askance on the great possible development of the fish trade.

In 1888 the steam trawler *Sybil* was acquired. Fishing boats from Brixham in Devon were regular visitors to the docks and, by 1904, Milford Haven had as many as sixty-six trawlers for deep-sea fishing and a hundred and fifty-four drifters for coastal fishing. By this time Milford Haven was the fourth most important fishing port in Britain after Grimsby, Hull and Fleetwood. As part of the development, a huge fish market was built on the quay, a building measuring 950 feet in length, with a railway running through it. The fish train would leave every day for Billingsgate market, and Milford Haven, perhaps for the first time in its history, was a busy and prosperous place.

However, this dream too was to be shattered. Since 1945, the fishing industry has declined, and is now almost completely in the hands of fishermen from France, Spain and Belgium, and there are no longer any fishing boats of any size owned by the inhabitants of the town. We can only speculate on the fate of the new marina set up in 1990-1992 to meet the needs of amateur sailors.

iv)   Haverfordwest

Bearing in mind the meandering nature of the Afon Cleddau Wen which flows through the town on its way to the sea, it is difficult to imagine that Haverfordwest, the county town of Pembrokeshire, was at one time one of the most significant ports in the west. The town was established around 1100 AD, when it became apparent that the hill above the Afon Cleddau was an ideal location to build a castle as a defence against the Welsh in the north, who were eager to protect their land from the Normans who had settled in southern Pembrokeshire. A small town grew up in the shadow of the castle, which brought in all its supplies from the sea.

However, it is the Flemish settlers who came to the area in the Middle Ages who are to be thanked for developing this important town on the Afon Cleddau. It was they who developed Haverfordwest as an industrial and trading centre. Wool, leather, and malt were all produced in the town and coal was exported from the quay. The Flemish settlers, who were such an influence on trade and industry in western Wales in the fourteenth and fifteenth centuries, were very suspicious of the Welsh, and for this reason they were keen to develop trade between Haverfordwest and continental Europe. Wine, salt, fruit and manufactured iron goods were imported to the Afon Cleddau from France, Spain and Portugal, and Haverfordwest became a very busy place. Until the mid-nineteenth century and the competition from the railway, there was a weekly service from the quay at Haverfordwest to the city of Bristol, and to this day the *Bristol Trader* pub reminds us of the importance of that commercial link.

Apart from being a market town serving an extensive area, Haverfordwest was also home to a large number of rural crafts supplying the needs of the area. There were saddlers, brewers, wheelwrights and blacksmiths, but perhaps the most important of all the town's industries was the *Llewellyn Churn Works*, which manufactured butter churns, cheese dishes and other essential commodities for the dairy industry. The Llewellyn works started off on a small scale as a cooper's workshop, but very rapidly came to supply the demand for dairy dishes from all parts of Britain, as was reflected in the exports from the port.

v) Pembroke and Pembroke Dock

In Pembroke one of the most magnificent of the Norman castles in southern Wales is situated on a hill above a branch of the Afon Cleddau. Although the town which grew up near the castle developed as a centre of seamanship, primarily as a place for the import of supplies for the Norman armies, the nature of the river made it quite unsuitable for large-scale commercial development, with mud and sand causing serious problems for shipping. Nevertheless, in the twelfth century, when the castle was at the height of its power, a number of rich noblemen took up residence in

Pembroke – among whom the most influential was, perhaps, Earl Gilbert de Clare, who passed legislation that every cargo vessel had to unload at the quay in Pembroke. Eventually, Pembroke lost this monopoly, although at one time the town possessed some two hundred ships that exported wool, leather, butter and fish, and imported wine, salt, tobacco, and many everyday commodities for the town and the surrounding area. In time, the waters under the castle were considered to be too shallow to be suitable for any but the smallest ships, and gradually the town lost its importance.

Things were very different a mile or so away downstream, where a unique town was to develop – Pembroke Dock. This was not a trade port, it would not become a ferry port until the mid-twentieth century, and nor was it a fishing port like Milford Haven on the other side of the Afon Cleddau. Pembroke Dock was a port which was constructed for a single express purpose: to build ships for the Royal Navy.

Pembroke Dock is unlike anywhere else in Wales, because this depressing town is the creation of a single industry and a single establishment. It was created by the Navy Board, and all its activities were associated with the building of warships. From 1814, when it was decided to move the shipyard from Milford Haven to Pembroke Dock, until 1926, when the yard was closed, a total of two hundred and sixty-nine ships were built there. The prosperity of Pembroke Dock is rather surprising, since the area had no useful raw materials. There were no iron or copper works or extensive forests for the provision of oak. Transport links between this corner of Wales and the rest of Britain and Ireland were impossible, nor did the area provide an inexhaustible pool of experienced labour. In fact the population density was low, and the only way to ensure an adequate workforce for the yards was by persuading people from other areas to migrate to Pembrokeshire. They came from all parts, and a large number of simple cottages, many of them single storey, were erected to house them. With so many strangers in town, it is hardly surprising that Pembroke Dock had a rather Wild West reputation.

For some sixty years, Pembroke Dock was considered to be the most important shipyard for building warships in Britain, and in order to protect this vital installation, a large number of defences, the Palmerston Forts, were built the length and breadth of the estuary from Pembroke Dock to the sea. As soon as iron became the main shipbuilding material – the era of the Ironclads, as they were known – the shipbuilding at Pembroke Dock was unable to exploit the new construction technology. There were no iron workers or foundries within a hundred miles. There was no longer any demand for the port to meet the fleet's needs for cruisers and battleships. Nevertheless, there was more demand in the yards for building smaller vessels, better suited for operations in shallow waters. These gunships consisted of wooden planks on iron frames and there was a considerable demand for them at the height of the British Empire. Five yachts were also built for the royal family here. However, slowly but surely, the activity created by Pembroke Dock was coming to an end, and very little other activity has taken its place. During the First World War a number of submarines were built at Pembroke Dock, but with the launching of the Fleet Auxiliary oil tanker the *Oleander* in 1926, the days of Pembroke Dock as a centre for shipbuilding were over.

The strangest development in Pembrokeshire in the nineteenth century was the construction of the large number of defensive forts between 1850 and 1870.

According to Lord Palmerston, Britain – and in particular the naval installation at Pembroke Dock – was in grave danger from the French navy, and defences had to be provided, at great cost, to counteract this threat. Some six forts were built along the southern coast of Pembrokeshire, such as St Catherine Island at Tenby, Lydstep and Caldey Island. There were nine others, although only one, Scaveston, was actually built on the banks of the Afon Cleddau, together with eight other forts and two Martello towers surrounded by water in the middle of the estuary. Several hundred soldiers could live in each fortress and the main purpose of these defences was to prevent attacks from the sea by French ships. This ambitious and rather peculiar strategy in its entirety was a complete waste of money and resources, but then the Cleddau estuary has witnessed many strange, extravagant and worthless schemes over the centuries.

vi)   St Brides Bay and Solva

The coastline of St Brides Bay in Pembrokeshire is among the most beautiful in the country. This is one of the main attractions of the Pembrokeshire National Park, and with its sprinkling of islands, such as Ramsey and Skomer not far offshore, and its little villages such as Marloes, St Brides, Little Haven, Broad Haven, Nolton, Newgale, Solva and Porth Glais, St Brides Bay has a lot to offer the visitor.

In the past, the seaside villages and magnificent beaches acted as landing places for the small ships and the numerous smugglers with their assorted cargoes. During the Dark Ages, Viking ships would come here on a regular basis, in particular to Porth Glais, in order to attack St David's.

By the end of the eighteenth century, the Pembrokeshire coalfield was producing anthracite for export all along the western coasts of Wales and Ireland. Some of the collieries, such as Nolton Haven, were located very close to the sea, and the workings extended far out under the waves. A tramway was built from another mine – the *Trefrân Cliff Colliery* – on the southern side of the superb beach at Newgale to allow the coal to be loaded on to the small ships. Coal from Little Haven colliery would also be exported from Newgale beach. Anthracite from Pembroke was considered to be of the highest quality, but due to enormous geological problems, the industry had disappeared before the end of the nineteenth century.

Of all the ports in St Brides Bay, the most important was Solva. Access to its sheltered and easily defended harbour was difficult, and involved a semi-zigzag course up the Afon Solfach. Certainly it provided a refuge from Viking raids during the Dark Ages. By the end of the sixteenth century Solva was starting to develop. John Leyland, the itinerant historian, described the harbour in 1530 as 'a small creek for balingers and fishing boats', while George Owen, the Pembrokeshire antiquarian, refers to it in 1603 as a 'portlet for small shipping'. Trade with Ireland was the mainstay of the port in the seventeenth century, and by the beginning of the eighteenth century, Solva was the main port in the bay. In 1756, a trading company was established in the village and nine large buildings were constructed on the banks of the river. The company acquired seven sloops, and all manner of cargo was imported to their warehouses. By 1840, the company was doing very well for itself and acquired four brigs, each of 200 tons, to carry goods from Solva to the Bristol Channel and to Bristol in particular. As many as twelve limekilns sprang up along the shoreline, and a number of small ships and boats were built here. Despite the village's commercial success in the nineteenth century – it had a population of 1,252 by 1851 – by 1901, the population had fallen to 730, and with the sinking of the last of the Solva steamships after it was torpedoed in 1915, the port that at one time had been so busy ceased to function.

vii)   Porth-gain and Aber-mawr

Between St David's and Fishguard lie a number of small coastal villages, each with a long history as a centre of seamanship. This is the area featured in the work of poets such as Crwys and Dewi Emrys, with their evocative lines to Melin Tre-fin and Pwllderi respectively. It is a remote and romantic area, imbued in many places with a strong sense of magic. The railway never reached this part of the country, and thus industrial developments over the years – in particular in stone quarrying at Abereiddi and Porth-gain – had to depend exclusively on maritime transport. In the era of railway fever during the latter half of the nineteenth century, Brunel and the railway authorities came up with ambitious plans to build a port at Aber-mawr and to transform the little hamlet of Abercastell into a transatlantic port of the same stature as Southampton and Liverpool. In the 1850s, northern Wales had its own major port at Holyhead with a daily ferry service to Ireland. But southern Wales did not, and in 1851 the lonely spot of Aber-mawr became a hive of activity, with numerous workers preparing for a harbour and a wide-gauge railway that would lead to Aber-mawr. However, despite the money already spent, Brunel decided to abandon the site and to build a railway and ferry port on the banks of the Afon Cleddau at Neyland.

Until the mid-nineteenth century, Abereiddi and Porth-gain were both very minor harbours, where the occasional cargo of lime or coal was brought in for the local population. Abereiddi is referred to as one of the main beaches for smuggling goods such as wine and salt. The area was found to have adequate deposits of slate and granite, and in 1849 three businessmen from London raised a lease on all the natural resources in the vicinity. A quarry was developed at Abereiddi, and nowadays this quarry, known as the Blue Lagoon, is one of the port's main attractions. However, because Abereiddi was located in such an exposed position, lashed by westerly gales, a narrow-gauge railway was soon built to Porth-gain a mile or so away, where a sheltered harbour was developed. At the turn of the twentieth century, the area was a hive of activity, but it was found that the local slate did not compare favourably with the slates from Cilgerran or those of northern Wales, and the industry rapidly went into terminal decline. The port was saved by the discovery of a rich bed of granite at Penclegyr. Mills were built on the quay at Porth-gain to crush the stone, and huge hoppers were built nearby for storing the crushed rock ready for export. With an adjacent brickworks, Porth-gain also produced stone slabs for the building of pavements and bridges.

Despite its narrow entrance, the port was extremely busy: steamships usually sailed on a daily basis, mainly to Bristol and the ports of the Bristol Channel, but also to Ireland and the north-west of England. After the First World War there were hard times, the result of competition from the more economical quarries in Europe. In 1929, the owners of Porth-gain – the *United Stone Firms* – went bankrupt and the last cargo was shipped out in 1931.

viii) Fishguard

The Afon Gwaun follows a short course, flowing swiftly from the Preselis into a sheltered bay. In contrast to the majority of Wales' western rivers, no sand bar has formed at its mouth. The waters rush through a narrow gorge and pour into the sea without slowing down. Because of the river's particular characteristics, salmon fishing has not developed at the mouth of the Afon Gwaun in the same way as it has in several other rivers in the west, such as the Afon Teifi and the Nyfer. When fishing did develop locally, it was for herring in the bay. According to George Owen, the county historian of the time, in the seventeenth century Pembrokeshire was 'inclosed with a sea of herrings'. Millions of fish would arrive in Fishguard during the autumn and the main occupation that developed at the mouth of the estuary was the harvesting, salting and smoking of these fish for export – particularly to Ireland. Transport between southern Wales and Ireland would dominate the entire development of Fishguard over the centuries that followed.

Fishguard was originally a small village with a bridge crossing the river, whose earliest history could be traced back to Viking times in the ninth and tenth centuries. Its inhabitants looked out to the open sea, and the steep-sided *cwm* presented an obstacle for any traffic and communication with its hinterland. In contrast to Cardigan, eighteen miles to the north, Fishguard was unable to take advantage of the industrial and agricultural produce of a wide area, which might have formed the basis of any export trade. With their sheltered harbour, the village of Wdig to the south and lower Fishguard in the north developed as centres of seamanship and, at the beginning of the nineteenth century in particular, these were communities whose whole livelihood revolved around the sea. The surrounding agricultural communities were unfamiliar and foreign to them.

In the seventeenth century, herring fishermen depended on ships from Ireland to carry their harvest to other ports, and a number of Irish merchants settled in the area. By the beginning of the eighteenth century, however, Fishguard was developing rapidly, and was second only to Haverfordwest as Pembrokeshire's most important port. An attempt was made to export slates from the quarries in the north of the county, despite the extreme difficulties in transporting them from remote quarries to the quayside at Fishguard. Salt fish and smoked fish were the main exports from the area. In 1808 Fishguard was described by *The Cambrian Travellers Guide* as being:

> A small town, the rugged and dirty streets of which are contrasted by the cottages being whitewashed not only upon the sides but the roofs also. The port is small but if assisted by a pier would be of admirable advantage to the Irish trade, as its situation to the north of Milford is calculated to render it a safer haven for ships, unable in blowing weather to get round St David's Head, and it is the only port on this coast not incommoded with shifting sands called a bar.

Fishguard, unlike ports such as Cardigan and Haverfordwest, was unable to exploit resources from a wide area; nevertheless, an important shipbuilding trade developed at the mouth of the river. Most of Fishguard's ships were small single-masted vessels – smacks such as the *Fidelity* (24 tons), the *William and Mary* (26 tons) and the *Rose* (36 tons). But as in nearby Newport, a number of schooners and brigs were built for sailing somewhat further than the coasts around Fishguard. It was here that schooners such as the *Maria and Martha* (96 tons) and the *Gwaun Maid* (117 tons) were built, and twin-masted brigs such as the *Gleaner* (133 tons), the *Martha* (156 tons) and the *Fortitude* (125 tons). The period between 1780 and 1840 was a prosperous time for Fishguard as a shipbuilding centre, and at least forty-five ships were built on the shores of the Afon Gwaun. After 1840, however, the port's shipowners came to rely on shipbuilders from other ports, including Newport and Cardigan, for ships to meet their requirements.

Of course, Fishguard was not primarily a centre for the export and import of goods, but instead became famous as a passenger port with important links to Ireland. Had some of the local traders had their way, Fishguard would, in fact, have developed as a passenger terminal for the United States. This was the dream shared by a number of individuals at the end of the nineteenth century.

One of the great problems facing the British government in the nineteenth century was the provision of a rapid and direct link between Britain and Ireland. To the administrators of law and order, governing this troublesome country was a most frustrating task. By 1850, Ireland was linked to Britain by means of the railway through northern Wales, by Telford's A5 road and by sea from Holyhead to Dublin. Southern Wales had no such link, and during the 1840s, under the guidance of the renowned engineer Isambard Kingdom Brunel, Fishguard Bay was earmarked as the most suitable location for building a port. The plan was to build a railway from London to Gloucester and on to Cardiff and from there to a huge maritime railway terminal at Aber-mawr or in Fishguard Bay.

However, despite all the early enthusiasm, Brunel's dream was never realised and in 1851 the scheme was shelved. By 1856 the port of Neyland – or New Milford Haven as it was called at that time – was the terminal for the *South Wales Railway*. Years would pass before the dream of developing Fishguard as the ideal passenger port would become a reality. First and foremost, such a port depended on a suitable and convenient railway link, and in 1876 the Maenclochog railway had come as far as the slate-quarrying village of Rosebush in the heart of the Preseli mountains. The line was extended as far as Treletert, and the idea was to extend it to Fishguard. Unfortunately, capital was in short supply, and by 1889 the unfinished railway was up for sale. A sales poster read:

> A line which though only short may ultimately become an important factor in Passenger and Goods Service between England and the South of Ireland. At the present time the whole of the north coast of Pembrokeshire from New Milford to Cardigan is unprovided with Railway Acommodation. The great importance of Fishguard in the character of a natural harbour and of Goodwich can hardly be exaggerated. The present local passage is from Milford to Waterford: a service if established between Fishguard and Waterford would be thirty five miles shorter.

In 1893, under the ownership of two businessmen from Birmingham and a group of Irishmen, the railway was built from Rosebush to Treletert and was opened in 1895. Four years later, the line from Treletert to Fishguard was completed. The line, which wound its way slowly through the Preselis, was completely unsuitable as a rapid transport link between London and Ireland. Within a short space of time, the *Great*

Western Railway had taken an interest in this less-than-successful venture, but the company was only interested in the section between Treletert and Fishguard. Millions were invested in building a new railway from Clarbeston Road station to Fishguard, and further millions were spent on preparing a new harbour at Wdig. In August 1906 a steamer service commenced between Fishguard Bay and Rosslare, a service that still flourishes to this day.

Because of the new port's success as the main link between Wales and Ireland, serious consideration was given to the idea that Fishguard might be developed like another Southampton or Liverpool into a port for transatlantic crossings. After all, said the optimists, Fishguard was the closest port in Britain to New York. In April 1908 ships of the *Booth Line* began to call in Fishguard on their passage from America, and on the 30th of August 1909 the *Mauritania* visited the bay. The *Lusitania* and the *Aquitania* also called there, and the link between Fishguard and New York remained until 1914. However, despite considerable sums of money being spent on the Ocean Quay, the ambitious dream to build another Southampton was over.

Despite the best efforts of the temperance movement in Wales, Cwm Gwaun inland from Fishguard is our most renowned area for the brewing of home ale. The *Hen Galan* festival [the old new year] is still celebrated in the valley and the beer is a vital component of these celebrations. In the past, *'macsu cwrw'* [brewing of beer] was an integral part of the work of almost every farmer's wife, and in this narrow valley there are still women who are considered experts in this ancient skill.

Despite a host of modern developments and an influx of outsiders, there is still something unchanging about Cwm Gwaun. It is an area of antiquities, where old festivals such as *Yr Hen Galan* thrive and where craftsmen and women still reside whose methods have changed little over many centuries.

ix) Newport

At the mouth of the Afon Nyfer [River Nevern] lies Newport, one of the oldest boroughs in western Wales, where to this day, members of the local 'Court Leet' and the 'Marcher Lord' play an important ceremonial (if not administrative) role in the town. The borough, built round the castle, has a long history of seamanship, and it is no wonder that Newport is twinned with the main US naval base in Annapolis. It was on the southern side of the river, in the tiny township of Parrog about half a mile from Newport, that the small port developed in the shadow of Pen Dinas. In the sixteenth century Newport was as important as Fishguard, and a report of 1566 refers to the trade between Newport and Bristol. In the eighteenth century, slates from Mynachlog-ddu and the Preselis were exported from Newport. Over the years, two limekilns and a number of warehouses were built at Parrog, and as was the case in every port throughout the world, the town had many pubs – as many as twenty-seven.

Strangely enough, a fair amount of shipbuilding activity took place along the river, and some of the vessels were quite substantial – the schooner *Agenoria* (117 tons) for example, which was built in 1834. The Havard family were the chief shipbuilders, and were kept extremely busy during the first half of the nineteenth century. The main vessels built at Newport were:

Adroit, 72-ton schooner – 1847
Agenoria, schooner modified as a brigantine – 1834
Alert, 33-ton sloop – 1835
Ann, 161-ton brig – 1842
Ann & Betty, 27-ton smack – 1837
Ann & Mary, 22-ton sloop – 1825
Ardent, 120-ton brig – 1826
Betty, 24-ton sloop – 1777
Brothers, 99-ton schooner – 1828
Charlotte, 81-ton schooner – 1825
Claudia, 135-ton schooner – 1835
Culloden, 83-ton brig – 1804
Diligence, 100-ton brig modified as a schooner
    – 1814
Elice, 145-ton brig – 1814
Elizabeth, 108-ton schooner – 1826
Elizabeth, 27-ton sloop – 1839
Elizabeth & Mary, 60-ton sloop – 1792
Ocean, 120-ton brig – 1832
Victory, 118-ton brig – 1811
Hope, 182-ton snow – 1827
Fanny Ann, 22-ton brig – 1801
Flora, 28-ton sloop – 1785
Harmony, 95-ton schooner – 1829
Hope, 21-ton sloop – 1805
Hope, 150-ton brig – 1823
Jane, 78-ton schooner – 1837
Jupiter, 64-ton sloop – 1802
Mary, 53-ton sloop – 1819
Mary Ann, 23-ton sloop – 1810
Minerva, 102-ton brig – 1842
Phoebe, 123-ton schooner – 1839
Reform, 14-ton sloop – 1831
Rose, 25-ton sloop – 1773
Swift, 39-ton sloop – 1825
Valiant, 144-ton brig – 1812

Venerable, 130-ton brig – 1815
William & Ann, 88-ton sloop – 1790

There was a strong tradition of seamanship here too, and until the mid-twentieth century a large number of men from Newport were seamen, many of them sailing on ships from Cardiff.

Among the small ports in this region of north Pembrokeshire was Pwll Gwaelod and Cwm yr Eglwys (where the church was largely destroyed in a huge storm in 1859). To the north between the rivers Nyfer and Teifi, there are high, steep cliffs, and the only landing place is Ceibwr and the village of Trewyddel, where some cargoes were landed, particularly *cwlwm* and limestone for burning in the kiln near the beach.

5.   CARDIGAN BAY – SOUTH

i)   Cardigan

The port of Cardigan was vital to the economic development of the Teifi valley and, up to the end of the nineteenth century, river traffic was immensely important, until the inconsiderate owners of Chwarel y Fforest blocked its passage by allowing waste to be tipped in the river. Even in 1878, the Lloyd family of Coedmor still considered river traffic to be of importance, and built a wharf near Rosehill farm. Boats were used 'for the purpose of carrying sand, coal, slate slabs, pipes, manure and any other material from Cardigan to Pwllnewydd under Coedmore'.

The end of the nineteenth century marked the certain end of a long era of economic development. Once the 'Cardi Bach' railway reached Cardigan in 1883, the demise of this key harbour was inevitable. Fifty years earlier, Cardigan had been one of Wales' main ports and the Customs Office in Stryd y Santes Fair controlled all the ports and shipping from Fishguard in the south, right up to Llanddewi Aber-arth in the north. Shipbuilding was also very important here: over two hundred ships were constructed on the banks of the Afon Teifi, both in Cardigan itself and at Llandudoch. In 1815, three hundred and fourteen ships were registered in the port; at the time, Cardigan had seven times as many ships as Cardiff, and three times as many as Swansea. Not only did ships from Cardigan sail the coasts of Britain and across to Ireland, but they also sailed to places as far away as America, Australia and the European continent. Emigration to north America from Cardigan was also very common, particularly during the period between 1820 and 1845. Famous ships such as the *Triton*, the *Albion* and the

Active transported hundreds of émigrés from western Wales in search of a better life in the United States and Canada. It is said that migrants on board the *Albion* were the first from Britain and Ireland to settle in Canada, and that New Cardigan in Fredericton, New Brunswick, commemorates those who, in a bid to escape the poverty and oppression back home in Wales, ventured the journey in such fragile ships across the Atlantic.

Even after the golden age of seamanship had come to an end at the end of the nineteenth century, the tradition continued in Cardigan, although few ships attempted to negotiate the sandbanks to sail into the town itself. A life at sea still attracted local youngsters, and right up to its last days as a port, engineers on some of the world's great ships could boast that they had been apprentices at one of the town's foundries, which were first established in conjunction with the shipbuilding and repair industry on the banks of the Teifi.

It was the broad stretch of water below the castle which was to see the greatest development, with the construction of a port that would eventually have international links. During the Middle Ages, there was a fair amount of traffic on the river, although most of the ships that came to Cardigan were of foreign origin. It was a risky business sailing in Cardigan Bay, which was subject to piracy but, little by little, Cardigan began to expand, and in 1199 received a charter.

Further improvement would follow the Acts of Union in the sixteenth century, as life in the region became somewhat more stable. A number of Navigation Acts were passed in an attempt to increase trade; efforts were also made to suppress piracy as well as to support coastal fishing. New and more effective methods of collecting tolls were introduced, and in this respect Cardigan would play a vital role. The golden age had dawned. Herring fishing quickly developed as one of the main local occupations and, during the Tudor period, ships from Ireland, France, England and Spain were regular visitors to Cardigan, picking up cargoes of salted and red herring for overseas. Some settled in the town, particularly merchants from Ireland, and it was they who were responsible for running the export trade from the harbour. Gradually, in addition to fish, goods such as Cilgerran slates, butter, grain, beer and wool were exported.

Despite their inherent reluctance to go to sea, other than to fish the coastal waters, Cardigan people saw their chance. By the early eighteenth century, the Afon Teifi had become extremely busy. Fish, agricultural produce, oak bark for the leather industry, and slates were all shipped from Cardigan, while an equally diverse range of goods was brought into the port, ranging from Spanish oranges to coal and building materials. By the end of the century, Cardigan had become a bustling, prosperous port with ships sailing all over the world.

Not only was Cardigan an outstanding port and a commercial centre for a wide area, but there was also major industrial development taking place in the town itself. There was a great demand for cargo ships and, as in many other places, shipbuilding became established along the Teifi to meet this demand. Until the early nineteenth century, it was mainly local timber, particularly from the Coedmor estate near Cilgerran, that was used for this purpose, but eventually ships from the Baltic and Nova Scotia would visit the port regularly, and before too long the shipbuilders came to rely on imported timber rather than on local produce. In 1839 shipbuilders were obliged to pay rent to the Town Council, and the records at this time show that the following individuals were working on the northern shore of the Teifi and at the mouth of Nant Mwldan: John Evans at Llandudoch, David Owen, Evan Morgan, and James and William James. By 1850 the industry was concentrated in three yards: Iard Uchaf at the mouth of the Mwldan, which belonged to David Owen; Iard Ganol on the site of the present-day car park and supermarket which belonged to Sam Evans, and a little further downstream Iard Isaf, which belonged to William Jones, a Methodist elder and preacher. One of William Jones' apprentices was John Williams, the last of the shipbuilders on the river, whose long career culminated with the launching of the *Margaret Ann* for John Parry of Tre-saith in 1877.

ii)   Aber-porth

Despite having a somewhat lesser status than Cardigan, the small villages of southern Cardigan, such as Aber-porth, Tre-saith and Llangrannog, have seen busy times as centres of seamanship. At the mouth of two streams – the Howni and the Gilwen – lie two beaches: Traeth Dolwen and Traeth y Dyffryn, or Traeth y Llongau. The sands of Traeth y Dyffryn stretch deep into the valley, creating a very sheltered harbour for shipping. In contrast with Llangrannog some four miles away, the shipbuilding industry never developed in Aber-porth. Only four small vessels were built there (*Jane* in 1787, *Brittania* and the *True Briton* in 1793, and the *Frances* in 1808). However, as a trade centre, Aber-porth was quite significant, and the villagers owned several small ships – some forty-eight ships in all between 1800 and 1870. Most of these were single-masted sloops, which carried *cwlwm* and lime to be burnt near the beach.

Typical of Aber-porth ships, indeed of ships in all the coastal villages, was the 40-ton smack, *Elizabeth Ann*, which was built in 1875 at John Williams' yard in Cardigan for John Morris, a seaman from Y Ddôl in Aber-porth. She was eventually wrecked on the beach at Aber-porth in 1892. Apart from John Thomas, who owned thirty-two shares (out of the sixty-four traditionally allocated to a ship), there were others such as the merchant Thomas Thomas of y Plas (with twenty-four shares), and farmers such as David Morgan, Trefere Bella and Mrs Elizabeth Jones, Troedyrhiw, who owned the remaining shares. Under the command of John Thomas of Y Ddôl, the *Elizabeth Ann* sailed regularly from Porthmadog and Caernarfon with a cargo of slates, and from Porth-gain to Gloucester with a cargo of stone, but most frequently to the ports of southern Pembroke and Carmarthen Bay to collect *cwlwm* and lime, which was landed at Aber-porth. It was the villagers – the *hobblers* – who were responsible for unloading the ships on the beach at Aber-porth, since each ship only carried a crew of three, and it was essential that every ship be unloaded quickly so that it could catch the next tide.

One of the most important activities to take place on the beach at Aber-porth was herring fishing, an occupation that continued at least up until 1914. Herring was vital to the economy of southern Cardigan, and salted and smoked fish was one of the area's few exports. In the early days boats from Ireland would come over to collect the barrels of fish in exchange for cargoes of salt and fishing gear from Ireland. Late in the eighteenth century, local ships and local seamen began to get involved in the herring export trade, and very quickly a maritime tradition grew up in villages such as Aber-porth and Llangrannog. The main occupation of the villagers was no longer merely catching Aber-porth herring, but also came to involve ocean sailing. The sea and maritime traffic became the mainstay of local employment, and although the maritime trade in Aber-porth itself would die out during the last quarter of the nineteenth century, sailing to all parts of the globe became a way of life for the villagers. In 1902, for example, the Calvinistic Methodist's Hen Gapel had a total of two hundred and forty-one members, and no less than twenty-seven of these were ships' masters, not to mention all the ships' engineers and seamen who were also members.

No wonder a number of the big shipping companies in Cardiff were able to trace their roots back to these little coastal villages in Cardigan.

One of the most successful of these was Evan Thomas, Dolwen, Aber-porth, son of Hezekiah Thomas, the owner of a small 47-ton ketch, the *Pheasant*, which, like the *Elizabeth Ann*, sailed along the western coasts carrying essential commodities for the coastal communities. Evan Thomas, however, went to Cardiff and sailed the ocean, becoming the master of one of *Henry Anning*'s tramp steamers, a company with roots in Devon. In 1881 he decided, together with one of *Anning*'s clerks – Henry Radcliffe from Merthyr – to set up a shipping company, and acquired the first ship, the *Gwenllian Thomas*, from the Palmer and James yard. This was soon followed by other ships, and by the time Evan Thomas died at the age of forty-nine in 1891, they owned fifteen ships. By 1913, *Evan Thomas Radcliffe* had as many as twenty-eight ships. This huge company, with all its world-wide connections, depended mainly on sailors from western Wales for its manpower. In 1890, for example, the captains of twelve of the company's eighteen ships came from Cardigan and northern Pembroke, and in fact a large proportion of the company's investors came from south-west Wales.

Among the captains employed by *Evan Thomas Radcliffe* in the 1890s were the two cousins from Aber-porth, James Jenkins of Frondeg and his brother-in-law David Jenkins of Bryntirion. The family was very busy with small ships that sailed from the beach at Aber-porth. However, James and David set off for Cardiff and established a new company, *Jenkins Bros*, in 1898-9, in partnership with W.J. Williams from Bethesda in Gwynedd. By 1900 the company had acquired seven ships, and a high proportion of their crews were from Cardigan, including their cousin Captain Daniel Jenkins of Brynberwyn, Tre-saith. Miss Anne Jenkins, a sister of James Jenkins of Frondeg, was responsible for recruiting boys from Aber-porth to work for the company, and it was not unusual for these young recruits to be driven in James' Rolls Royce to their ships in Cardiff. Members of the Jenkins family were also responsible for establishing the breakaway chapel at Bryn Seion in Aber-porth and were its main benefactors.

There are times when it is prudent to buy and invest in shipping, and *Evan Thomas Radcliffe* and *Jenkins Bros* were lucky enough to develop their businesses during the shipping boom of the last two decades of the nineteenth century and the early years of the twentieth. By 1903, however, the tide had turned, and other companies were less successful. In that year the *Glanhowny Steamship Company Ltd* was set up by Captain Thomas Owen of Glanhowny, Aber-porth and Henry Bartlett from Cardiff. They bought the *Bala*, one of *Radcliffe*'s old ships, and re-named it the *Glanhowny*. Following the death of Captain Owen in 1906, a second vessel was acquired, the *Barto*, the old *Mary Thomas*. The company's history is somewhat murky with respect to the *Glanhowny*, which was insured for

£13,126 – rather more than the £8,000 or so which was paid for her. Subsequently, the ship sank somewhere between Carloforte and Antwerp in May 1907. By 1909 the company was bankrupt and one of the owners complained that they were 'absolutely without funds. There is not one penny with which to do anything'.

Another of the Aber-porth companies, that of Captain Daniel Jenkins, who was the brother of Captain David Jenkins of the successful *Jenkins Bros*, suffered a similar fate. 1903 saw the establishment of the *Aber-porth Steamship Company*, which purchased another of *Radcliffe*'s old ships, the *W.J. Radcliffe*, renamed the *Aberporth*. She did not last very long, sinking in the Black Sea in June of that year, within sight of the shore. It soon became apparent that she had been insured for £5000 in excess of her value.

Over the years, the port of Aber-porth played a vital role in the maritime history of Wales. For centuries, herring from Aber-porth had been fundamental to the development of the sea trade. Ships from the Aber-porth area were to be seen all around the coasts and ports of Wales and, following the disappearance of the small ships, Aber-porth became the breeding ground for generations of sailors and masters who would sail far from home. Many of the world-renowned Cardiff shipping companies also originated from Aber-porth. In the prosperous days of the small ships, it was also the administrative headquarters of the *Aberporth Mutual Ship Insurance Company*, which was responsible for underwriting ships from Cardigan to Aberaeron.

iii) Tre-saith

Tre-saith is a small village lying slightly to the north of Aber-porth. However, in contrast to Aber-porth and

Llangrannog to the north, Tre-saith is not a particularly old village. Towards the end of the nineteenth century, a flour mill stood above the magnificent waterfall that pours into the sea from the Afon Bern, and there was a row of cottages known as 'The Barracks', which were home to the coastguards. There was also an inn called *The Ship*. Although Tre-saith – or Traeth-saith as it is occasionally called – was the site of a limekiln and a *cwlwm* yard, there was little development here prior to the end of the nineteenth century. A visiting journalist from Cardigan went as far as to describe Tre-saith as 'a second Brighton'. During the final decade of the century, there was extensive building work, and the village and its surroundings became a popular holiday venue. The little chapel of Hermon had to be built to accommodate the visitors, although this establishment never really did very well.

Long before the days of the holiday village, the sheltered beach at Tre-saith had acted as a small harbour, and the Parry family at *The Ship* owned a ship that was employed locally to bring in agricultural and domestic supplies.

A small amount of shipbuilding took place here, and in 1785 the 20-ton smack *Nancy* was built on the beach. In 1827, John Parry from *The Ship* built another smack – the 25-ton *Hope* – which sank near Ynys Dewi in 1845. Following this tragedy, a ship – the *Ruth* – was acquired from New Quay and for a quarter of a century this vessel traded along the whole length of the coast. The most famous of the ships belonging to John Parry and his son Evan was the *Margaret Ann*, built by John Williams of Cardigan in 1877. Apart from the daily trade in lime and *cwlwm* to Tre-saith, this ship sailed once a year to Connah's Quay on the Dee to collect a cargo of crockery, bricks and water pipes from the Bwcle potteries, which would be sold at the China

Store in Llangrannog (on the site of the present-day Glynafon stores). To the villagers of Llangrannog the *Margaret Ann* was known as *Y Llong Lestri* (the china ship) and sailed on a regular basis until 1918, when she sank near Fishguard.

iv)   Penbryn

Looking at golden Penbryn beach, full of summer visitors, it is hard to believe that this area was once the site of a very different form of activity. Many years ago, Penbryn was a favourite haunt of smugglers running salt and other contraband goods, which they landed on the beach at the dead of night. To this day, the narrow valley which leads from Llanborth to the sea is known as Cwm Lladron [*the Robbers' Valley*] because along its narrow track, local people would bring heavily laden carts full of contraband from Ireland. In addition to salt, there would be wine from Bordeaux and liquor from Dublin. It is not surprising that, on a visit to the area in 1743, the Methodist preacher, Howell Harris would comment on the inhabitants' 'Cheating the king of goods excised' and their 'inhuman behaviour toward poor shipwreckedseamen'. My ancestors were obviously a dreadful lot.

From the sixteenth century onwards, the main occupation of those living on the coast was herring fishing, and a lot of fish was exported to Ireland. For a long time it was Irish vessels that would bring the barrels and salt for salting the fish, because the inhabitants of southern Cardigan were unwilling to sail too far out of sight of land. The beach at Aber-porth and the beach at Penbryn, along with Cardigan, were the main ports for the herring trade and there was no mention of Llangrannog, Tre-saith, Cwmtydu or New

Quay. Gradually, however, local people became interested in sailing further than within sight of land, and slowly but surely the Cardi began to replace the Irishman as the sea trader. To the inhabitants, the sea became a thoroughfare rather than a barrier. My great-great-grandfather, David, for example, was an unnoteworthy day labourer, who scratched a living from about six acres of land at Plasbach near Melin Llanborth. He also did a bit of herring fishing, but at some point around 1770, David began to venture further and would spend the summer months sailing to Ireland to sell salted herring in Wicklow. On one of his voyages he brought back a wife with him to Plasbach – Hannah Christmas. David was a part-time sailor who farmed a little, fished a little and occasionally sailed across the Irish Sea. His son Joseph was somewhat different. He was a man of the sea, and was the single owner of a small sloop called *Rachel*, which he would use to bring *cwlwm* from Pembrokeshire and lime from Caldey Island to Penbryn. Around 1840, Joseph moved with his family from Plasbach to the village of Llangrannog, which at the time was in its heyday as a port. He lived in a thatched cottage, Y Rhip, until he moved to Rock Terrace in the 1870s.

Near the beach at Penbryn there was a limekiln and a village that had grown up around the mill near the old mansion of Llanborth. On a piece of ground near Penllain Maesglas (now known as Manorafon), the 24-ton sloop, the *Blessing*, was built in 1770, and not far away there was a woollen mill that produced flannel cloth for the local population. Until the vicarage was built by the Rev. John Hughes in the 1840s, an inn and brewery occupied the site at Troedyrhiw (this was in the days before the temperance movement). With its mill, kiln, workshops for a range of craftsmen, church and school, the area around Traeth Penbryn was almost self-sufficient.

The sea was the key element in everyone's lives. On moonlit evenings in the summer, groups of people would go digging for sand-eels. Limpets and mussels were collected, and the variety of techniques involved in the salting and smoking of herring were very familiar to the local women. Occasionally, the sea would provide an unexpected harvest, such as on the evening in December 1816 when a French ship seeking shelter in Aber-porth was wrecked on the rocks at Gaerlwyd beach. The ship was carrying a cargo of French wine, which was a great boon to the locals. Unfortunately, the binge drinking that ensued claimed the lives of seven of the local inhabitants.

Although by 1830 Penbryn was in rapid decline as a trade centre, owing to the development of Aber-porth and Llangrannog, a number of local inhabitants were still shipowners up until the end of the century. The family at Treddafydd owned a large number of shares in the schooner *Jessie* (75 tons), and a member of the family, John Griffiths of Sarnau – *Y Capten Bach* – was her master. The family at Ffynnon-wen owned the schooners *Cleddau Bell* (114 tons) and *Leander* (59 tons), and the owners of a number of ships from both Aber-porth and Llangrannog were from Penbryn.

v) Llangrannog

When you look at Llangrannog today, it is easy to assume that the houses around the beach are the true heart of the village. Until the mid-eighteenth century however, there was no mention of any sort of village at the water's edge. It seems probable that the first dwelling to be built near the beach was *The Ship and Anchor*, or Eisteddfa House, built in around 1760 by John Griffiths, the youngest son from Eisteddfa farm.

He married Catherine Davies from Penbryn and, in contrast with the rest of his family, he was attracted by the sea, and within a few years was the owner of some eight small ships that sailed from the cove at Llangrannog. Gradually, a small cluster of houses grew up around the beach, which became known as Beach Village or Y Tra'th during the nineteenth century.

However, there is a Llangrannog more ancient than Y Tra'th. This is the settlement established in the sixth century by Carantoc, an itinerant monk who made his way along the coasts of western Europe, founding religious centres close to the sea. Carantoc is said to have been an uncle of Saint David and lived sometime between 500 and 548 AD. He set up a religious cell at Leon in Brittany, at Crantock in Cornwall, and at Carhampton in Somerset. He was the leader of a number of other itinerant saints such as Cubert and Tenan, who travelled by sea rather than overland. Every church that he established lies near the sea, and yet cannot actually be seen from it, and the flat land above the Gerwn was a perfect site for establishing his church at Llangrannog. It could be that the saint's original shelter was in the cave above the modern-day graveyard, where he would at least have been safe from the pirates who habituated the coast of Ceredigion.

In time, a church was indeed built on this stretch of land, and gradually a settlement grew up around it. Games would be played below the walls of this church, and on the saint's day, May 16th, this is where the fair would be held. This event continued up until the beginning of the nineteenth century, when it was moved to the turnpike road. Here it continued until some forty years ago as the Ffair Glangaea [Halloween Fair] of New Inn. Probably the old church village had its own community. There was a flour mill and an inn

at Dolmeddyg. The last innkeeper was David Jones –
Dafi Doctor – whose claim to fame was his having
transported a shipload of eggs from Llangrannog to
Liverpool without a single breakage. Below Y Gerwn
was the wool factory which operated until 1912,
producing tweed and blankets for local people. Saint
Carantoc's church was rebuilt in 1885, and the first
baptism to take place in the new building was that of
my father, David James Jenkins from Troedrhiwgam.

The church has an interesting connection with Peter
Williams, a religious commentator and one of the
leaders of the Methodist Revival, who was a curate
there for a while. One day there was a scrap between
him and the parish rector, but Peter Williams claimed
that he was strong enough at that time to hold his own
against the rector and, although the latter grabbed hold
of his collar and tried to prevent him from entering the
pulpit, Williams managed to preach a powerful
sermon. Unfortunately, he was obliged to leave
Llangrannog the following day. Another rector of
Llangrannog, the Reverend Eleazer Evans, was a
victim of harassment at the time of the Rebeca Riots,
and received threatening letters for having built a
church school near Llangrannog. 'I heard about you,'
says the author of one of the letters,

> that you have been very dishonest with regard to
> the building, and that you have portrayed it as a free
> school for the people, and that you have turned it
> into a church and that you get £80 a year for your
> service. If this is true, you must give every last
> halfpenny of the money back . . . I will come with
> 500 or 600 of my daughters to pay you a visit and to
> destroy your property five times over and to make
> you an object of shame in the eyes of the whole
> community. I am against oppression. We remain
> yours, Rebeca and her daughters.

In a primarily Methodist community such as Llangrannog, with an early history of *seiad* meetings, what is surprising is that the Bancyfelin chapel was not in fact opened until 1863. The chapel was again located in the old church village and, indeed, 'Y Pentre' as opposed to 'Y Traeth' was the social centre until about a hundred years ago.

Things were changing rapidly along the coast of southern Ceredigion some two hundred years ago. Until then, it had been a purely agricultural area, although some more daring individuals would venture out during the autumn to fish for herring, which was common in Cardigan Bay. As soon as the call of the bird known as 'Guto Gruglwyd' was heard towards the end of August or beginning of September it meant the herring season had arrived (the identity of this bird is unknown). These fishermen were people of the land who ventured out in their fragile boats from local beaches. The fish was so abundant that it was impossible to use it all locally, and gradually a trade developed, exporting salted or smoked herring from the beaches of Ceredigion. Unfortunately, the Cardi wasn't much of a seaman until the mid-eighteenth century and it was boats from Ireland that would come to collect the sea's harvest. These boats would also bring the essentials of the fishing trade, such as nets, barrels and salt, which they would land at Cardigan, Aber-porth or on the beach at Penbryn. There is no mention of Llangrannog as a landing place until the mid-eighteenth century and at that time only the village around the church was in existence.

Times changed and the Cardi began to take an interest in seamanship as well as in fishing, and he saw that he too could participate in the sea trade which, up till then, had been monopolised by the Irish. Members of farming families began to acquire small ships, not just for the export of herring but also for the import of essential supplies. There was John Griffiths, for example, the youngest son from Eisteddfa, and Thomas Oliver from northern Pembrokeshire and his wife, Ann, who arrived in the village in 1762. Oliver built himself a house and gave it the somewhat grandiose name of *The Hall*, although it became known as *Y Rhal* in popular speech. Oliver was also a mariner and owned ships, and a considerable amount of land below the Gerwn waterfall in Llangrannog. The builder of the *Ship Inn* was also a sailor, as was the majority of the population in the settlement, which spread rapidly by the water's edge between 1760 and 1840.

At the beginning of the nineteenth century, Llangrannog was at its height, and the whole way of life of the new village was tied up with the sea and its trade. There were now four limekilns (the fifth, which is still to be seen, was built by Morgan Jenkins of Morfa Uchaf, as recently as 1887) and it is to these kilns that lime from Caldey Island, southern Pembroke and the Gower was brought to be burnt in order to make fertiliser for the land. Ships would come with cargoes of *cwlwm* from Hook, Penbre and Swansea, and at Glynafon there was the china emporium where pottery from Bwcle was sold. There was also an important boat yard here, and between 1787 and 1859 as many as fifteen ships were built, ranging from the little 7-ton *Linnet*, to the enormous *Ann Catharine*, a brig weighing 211 tons.

The village of Llangrannog attracted seamen from other areas, such as my great-grandfather, Joseph Jenkins, who was born in the smallholding at Plasbach near Melin Llanborth in 1820. Joseph sailed his small ship, the *Rachel*, from the beach at Penbryn, but after marrying, he moved to the village of Llangrannog. Joseph was a real sailor and, unlike his father, he had no interest whatsoever in agriculture; an acre of land and a cow at Plasbach meant little to him. A stalwart of Bancyfelin chapel and the Pentre Arms alike, he spent his whole life sailing the coasts in his *Rachel* and *Mari Fach*.

The brig, the *Ann Catharine*, was a large vessel, larger than any other ship that came to the beach to unload lime and *cwlwm*. In fact, the *Ann Catharine* only saw the beach at Llangrannog once, and that was in 1859 when she was being built in the yard at the *Ship*. She was a square-rigged two-masted vessel, 103 feet in length, 25 feet broad and 13.5 feet in height, and according to Lloyd's list, she weighed 211 tons. Not only was she the largest ship ever to be built at Llangrannog, but she was also the largest to be owned by local shipmasters. The finest timber from the Bronwydd estate was used to build her, and the iron for the anchors and the sails were made by the craftsmen of New Quay. Built in the yard at the *Ship*, she had to be dragged to New Quay to be completed by these renowned and skilled workers. On the 6th of August 1859, the ship, with a crew of nine, set sail on her maiden voyage in ballast from New Quay to Cardiff.

The owner of the *Ann Catharine* was Captain James Lloyd of the *Ship*, who was also the owner of a much smaller vessel – the sloop *Susannah Gwenllian*, which was built at New Quay in 1854. Without doubt, James the Ship was quite a character, who was willing to invest everything he owned, as well as his neighbours' cash, in the shipping trade. Of the sixty-four shares traditionally allocated to a ship, James Lloyd owned fourteen shares in the *Ann Catharine*, and his brother Evan just one. There were twenty-one other shareholders involved, most of whom were farmers from the Pontgarreg area. In the list of owners there were also individuals such as Samuel Morris, a tanner from Rhydlewis, and Josiah Jones, from the shop at Pontgarreg. Initially, James Lloyd had no shipmaster's certificate, which he needed for deep-sea sailing, following the passing of the Merchant Shipping Act of 1854. He therefore had to appoint Captain Daniel Rees of Dolhawen as master of the *Ann Catharine*. Captain Rees was described as 'Sailing Master' and James Lloyd as 'Business Master', and the entire crew came from the Llangrannog area. Among them was Simon Jones, Evan Bowen, Evan Evans, David Evans, John Davies and two boys, Thomas Evans (latterly Capt. Evans, Blaenwaun) and John Jones (latterly Capt. Jones, Brynaeron).

On the 14th of September 1859, the *Ann Catharine* set sail on a voyage from Cardiff with a cargo of coal for Alicante in Spain, and arrived after a smooth passage lasting three weeks. After three weeks in Alicante, she sailed to Palermo in Sicily, and although this was a voyage of over seven hundred miles, the *Ann Catharine* managed to complete it in four days. From there, the ship sailed to Catania and then followed a long haul back to Glasgow, reaching the river Clyde on the 9th of January 1860.

It is surprising to think that a ship, built by craftsmen in the yard of the *Ship* on the little beach at Llangrannog, sailed as far as the Mediterranean. Curiously, I have in my possession a diary of that voyage kept by Simon Jones, a member of the crew. On the voyage, he saw sights such as Mount Etna, and having been raised in the Sunday School tradition, he was aware that he was following one of the journeys made by the Apostle Paul.

However, if the first voyage was comparatively straightforward, the second was a rather different affair, since this time the *Ann Catharine* was to cross the Atlantic and to go as far as Buenos Aires and Rosario in south America. This was a voyage that lasted some eight months, and Simon Jones was surely glad to be able to spend a day in a missionary church in Rosario on the 5th of August 1860. The voyage from south America to Liverpool was an extremely hazardous one, but they reached their destination safely.

In the years that followed, the *Ann Catharine* crossed the Atlantic on several occasions, carrying coal from Cardiff and fish from Newfoundland to the Mediterranean. In 1873, however, this ship from Llangrannog undertook a long voyage lasting three years. A cargo of rails was taken on board in Swansea, which were to be used on the new East African railway. Unfortunately, after having discharged this cargo at Lourenco Marques, there was no cargo available for the *Ann Catharine*. Therefore James Lloyd sailed back across the Atlantic, a voyage which lasted some four months, and reached Galveston in the United States. There they picked up a cargo of cotton for Liverpool. After two years, the crew were at last on their way home. Unfortunately, however, on a stormy night in February 1876, the ship struck the rocks near Aberffraw on the western coast of Anglesey, and that was the end of the last ship to have been built on the beach at Llangrannog. Fortunately, all the crew was saved.

vi)   Cwmtydu

Between Llangrannog and New Quay, the cliffs rise steeply from the sea and, apart from the village of Cwmtydu, there are only seabirds, seals and dolphins here. No wonder that this part of the Ceredigion coast has been designated as an Area of Special Scientific Interest. Not far from Llangrannog, in a sheltered part of the coastal marshland, the Welsh youth organisation the Urdd has one of its main facilities, which has attracted generations of youngsters to enjoy the resources it offers. Not far from the Urdd centre near Trwyn Croi, an attempt was made to find and exploit lead deposits. In 1865, a large quantity of ore was mined from Pwll y Mwyn and exported to Swansea in a 35-ton smack from Llangrannog. Unfortunately, the ship sank before leaving Llangrannog, and that spelled the end of an industry which a small group of entrepreneurs had hoped would bring them wealth.

Cwmtydu is a small, remote village that consists of little more than the *Glanmorllyn* pub and a few cottages and therefore hardly deserves to be called a village. It is accessed by means of a narrow, winding valley from Llwyndafydd, and despite its remote location, it was the site of a limekiln and a fair bit of maritime traffic until about 1900. One small ship was built here, the *Ledney*, in 1786, and during the last quarter of the nineteenth century, ships such as the *Antelope*, the *Martha Jane*, the *Mari Fach*, the *Gwendolen* and the *Christianna* would unload *cwlwm* and lime on the sheltered beach. Cilie farm, home to a famous family of poets was not far from Cwmtydu and when the *Antelope* sank near the beach in June 1897, one of them, Jeremiah Jones, was ready with his verse:

Yr *Antelope* druan enillodd ei chlod
Wrth ddwyn marsiandaeth i hafan ddi-nod,
Gorffennodd ei gyrfa mewn storom go gas
Aeth hithau yn yfflon ar drwyn Cafan Glas.

Dihangodd y morwyr o ddannedd yr aig
Gan ddringo fel cathod dros gribyn y graig,
Os methodd morwriaeth ni chollwyd y criw,
Aeth pawb yn ddihangol a'r capten yn fyw.

Bydd effaith y storom ar drêd Mari Fach
A chyll y gwerinwr ei gwlwm du bach,
Daw'r gaeaf cynddeiriog i fwthyn a phlas
Ar 'Ante' yn huno ym medd Cafan Glas.

The poor old Antelope *much praised in her day*
For bringing trade to many a creek and bay
Met her end in dreadful gales
Smashed on Cafan Glas point on the coast of Wales

The crew escaped from the ocean's maul
Climbing like cats up a sheer rock wall
Though seamanship failed in that terrible gale
The captain and crew all lived to tell the tale.

Mari Fach's trade will suffer from this
The black cwlwm *fuel we'll all sorely miss*
There's a hard winter ahead in both hovel and plas
With the Ante *sleeping in its grave at Cafan Glas.*

Why there were celebrations and a *noson lawen* on Cwmtydu beach after the sinking, nobody knows, but one thing is certain: there was little evidence of any activity on the beach after the accident – if it was an accident. Around 1908, however, there was something of a revival in trade from the beach, such that Jeremiah Jones declared:

Mae traethell fach Cwmtydu
Yn codi i'w ail fri
Trwy ddod â'r llong Christianna
A llwyth o gwlwm du.
The little cove at Cwmtydu
Is seeing a second boom
With the arrival of the Christianna
And its cargo of pure black cwlwm.

One of the most remarkable stories concerning the

lonely beach at Cwmtydu is that German submarines used to anchor there during the First World War. It is alleged that their crews came into contact with a number of local people in the pub at Glanmorllyn, and took fresh water to the U-boats.

vii)   New Quay

As a busy summer holiday resort, with caravans covering large swathes of the coast and pleasure craft filling the harbour, it is difficult to believe that New Quay, whose whole way of life is now inextricably bound to the tourist and leisure industries, was at one time one of the most important shipbuilding ports in Wales. Over two hundred and fifty ships, both large and small, were built here to sail all over the world. Sailing was also the main occupation for the majority of its male population, and the British Merchant Navy employed a considerable number of New Quay boys, some of whom reached the highest echelons of their profession.

Strangely enough, New Quay is a comparatively recent settlement: up until 1835 there is no mention of it on any map or chart. There was, of course, a parish church located at Llanllwchaearn and another to the north at Llanina, and there were one or two cottages down at the water's edge which were home to a handful of fishermen. The wharf at Penpolion provided some shelter from the wind, but it was not much more than a few piles driven into the sand and held in place by rocks. As early as 1700, this insignificant landing place was described as 'the New Key', but was actually no more than a rudimentary shelter for local herring fishing boats. By the end of the eighteenth century, there were a number of local

fishermen and farmers who had invested in ships –
smacks such as the *Speedwell*, the *Catherine*, the *Saviour*,
the *Arthur*, the *Marie* and the *Hopewell*, mainly from the
port of Cardigan. By the end of the eighteenth century,
there was a fresh, enterprising spirit in the region when
one of Ceredigion's leading agricultural pioneers,
Lewis Turnor of Wervillbrook, Pentregât, became keen
to develop a harbour in order to export agricultural
produce from south Ceredigion to all parts of the
country, and in particular to Ireland. Turnor believed
that Cei was the best location for the development of a
ferry port to Ireland and was genuinely convinced that
it was a far better site for development than either
Holyhead or Milford Haven. His scheme failed and
New Quay had to wait another century before
someone else came along to promote the idea of
developing a major port.

Captain Longcroft of Llanina was very eager to see
the development of a transatlantic port at New Quay,
and he and a group of ambitious friends were prepared
to invest £30,000 in a scheme to build a new
Southampton near Carreg Ina at Cei-bach. This
ambition is reflected in a piece of poetry by Rees Jones
(Amnon) from Llandysul:

Cei Newydd ddaw'n ariannog, cyn bo hir,
Ei borthladd fydd ardderchog, cyn bo hir,
Daw iddo'r llongau mwya'
Yn llwythog o Jamaica,
A ffrwythau rhandir India,
Hwn fydd gogoniant Gwalia
Cyn bo hir.

New Quay will get rich very soon,
It'll have a splendid harbour very soon,
It'll attract the biggest ships

With cargoes from Jamaica,
And fruit from distant India,
It'll be the glory of Gwalia
Very soon.

The Llandysul rhymester's predictions were never realised, as one of the prerequisites of a large port was a railway and road system. There was heated debate among those who wanted to see a railway link to an enormous depot near Cross Inn, which would run from Newcastle Emlyn to Gogerddan and Brynhoffnant, or from Henllan to Rhydlewis and Ffostrasol, or along the Cletwr valley through Talgarreg, or from Llanybydder to Mydroilyn and Llanarth. In 1885, a decision was made to ask two engineers, Stephen Evans and J.W. Szlumper, to undertake what would now be termed a feasibility study. Despite the endless arguments between the inhabitants of Ffostrasol and Talgarreg, the line from Llandysul to New Quay through Ffostrasol won the day. An appeal was made for £36,000 in capital to complete the project, but no investors came forward and so the dream of ocean-liners evaporated.

The catalyst for the creation of New Quay was the *New Quay Harbour Act* of 1835, when permission was granted for the construction of a pier as a shelter for ships. This part of the Ceredigion coastline was to change spectacularly and now became something more than the 'resort of small fishing vessels', as it had been described in 1748 by Lewis Morris, the renowned antiquarian and surveyor from Anglesey. There had been a huge growth in demand for ships to export the manufactured goods of industrial Britain to all parts of the world and to import essential commodities even to the remotest locations. By the early decades of the nineteenth century, the ship building industry was well and truly established on the open beaches and in the

villages and towns of western Wales. Between 1780 and
1810, twelve sloops were built for farmers and
shopkeepers in the New Quay area. These were mostly
small vessels to meet local needs. In time, however,
some of the farmers extended their interests and began
to concentrate on shipownership. John Owen, for
example, had a small farm at Cilie, and used the little
smack *Ellen* to import *cwlwm* and lime to New Quay.
Within a few years he owned the *Ellen Owen* (132 tons),
Ellen (68 tons), *Heather Bell* (258 tons), *Heedfull* (92 tons),
James and Mary (86 tons) and the *Owney Belle* (127 tons).
Unfortunately, John Owen was rather too ambitious,
and by 1880 his venture had failed and his ships were
being sold off.

During the second half of the nineteenth century, the
shipowners of New Quay were both numerous and
successful, particularly those who invested in large
vessels that sailed all over the world, but which never
came anywhere near New Quay. Although a number of
ships belonging to people from New Quay were built
on local beaches, in particular those built by Evan
Daniel at Cei-bach, in time owners invested in cheap
ships built in Canada. These didn't last very long: the
407-ton barque the *Annie Ramsey*, for example, which
was built in 1863, was lost in 1867, and the 293-ton brig
the *Maggie Cummins*, which was built in Prince Edward
Island in 1873, was lost in the Gulf of Mexico in 1880.

By 1870, New Quay was a first-rate maritime
community, with a total of thirty-seven families
running a large fleet of ships of all sizes throughout the
world, usually crewed by sailors from New Quay itself.
Perhaps the most famous of all the New Quay ships
was the 189-ton brig *Hetty Ellen*, which was built at
Llanelli in 1860. She was bought by the family of David
Davies who had owned three ships – the *Hetty Mary*,
the *Nymph* and the *Pacific* – and sailed under the

command of David Davies with a crew of nine. The *Hetty Ellen* was commissioned by the agent of Dr David Livingstone, and arrived in South Africa in 1861. From Durban she sailed to the Zambezi, where she landed essential supplies for the famous missionary and explorer. The ship was lost without trace on a voyage to Nova Scotia in 1881.

As was the case in every other village along the coast of Cardigan Bay, the local shipping trade had almost entirely disappeared by the end of the nineteenth century. Although the railways and roads had replaced ships, the maritime tradition remained alive in New Quay. A large proportion of local young men still went to sea, and New Quay's link with Liverpool was particularly strong. In today's holiday resort, the relics of the old activity are still to be seen. There are two or three warehouses, the remains of a rope-yard and a sailmaker's workshop, as well as the customs offices – all of which are now hotels or chip shops. Here and there, the names of local ships are to be found in house names – the *Araminta* and the *Ina Lass*, the *Renown* and the *Albion* – which reminds us of the maritime heyday of the coastal villages of Ceredigion.

viii) Cei-bach

The open beach at Cei-bach, surrounded by caravan parks, has changed beyond recognition since the nineteenth century. There is very little evidence to suggest that this remote beach was one of the most prominent shipbuilding centres along the shores of Cardigan Bay. Of course, ships could be built anywhere where the land was comparatively flat and where there was a certain amount of shelter from the prevailing winds. A sawpit was needed, where it was possible to cut the oak into the correct size and shape, and some sort of building to assemble the timber. A forge was also required to produce the ironwork, but there was no need for any complicated dry dock.

Strangely enough, the annual *Lloyd's Register of Shipping*, which records the location where every ship in the world is built, differentiated between 'New Quay' and 'Q-bach'. Cei-bach was important enough to be recorded in the Registers as a shipbuilding centre. From 1814 until 1882, the beach was a hive of activity, and there were at least five builders at work during this period. Perhaps the most famous of these was Thomas James Thomas, who worked from 1850 until his death in 1866, and who was responsible for building magnificent ships that travelled regularly all over the world. Among them were the schooner *Maelota* and the brig *Cambria*, both of which sailed across the Atlantic on a regular basis to Newfoundland, to bring salt fish from Newfoundland to Italy and Spain. They would then return to Canada with a cargo of wine and olive oil.

Evan Daniel was an apprentice to Thomas Thomas and became a builder of considerable note. From 1855 until his death in 1890, Evan was kept very busy, and was renowned throughout Wales for building large ocean-going vessels. In 1872, for example, he built the 180-ton barquentine *Nymph*, which was wrecked in Bordeaux in 1886. In 1878 he built the *Maggie Phillips*, a brigantine of 165 tons, which was wrecked on a lonely beach in Brazil seven years later.

Between New Quay and Cei-bach there is an open beach known as Traeth-gwyn. It was the site of a sizeable settlement until the sea eroded the land. This spot was also important to shipbuilding in the area. At least seven shipbuilders operated there, all of whom, with the exception of Owen Owens, bore the name Davies. Between 1835 and 1866, for example, Thomas Davies and his son John built a large number of ships, including the *Hawendale*, one of the largest of Llangrannog's ships, and the schooner *U. Larsing*.

A huge caravan park is now located above the sea at Traeth-gwyn. Long-forgotten vessels such as the *Sylph*, the *Clarita*, the *Julianna* and the *Melodia*, which brought so much fame and fortune to this remote beach, are probably of little interest to the present-day visitors who flock here in their thousands every summer.

ix) Aberaeron

Today Aberaeron is home to the headquarters of Ceredigion County Council. It is a charming town with its carefully designed Georgian terraces, and is a fitting memorial to the Reverend Alban Thomas Jones Gwynne, who created the new harbour there between 1807 and 1811. As if that weren't enough, it was also he who was responsible for developing New Quay some four years later in 1815. He employed a stonemason called William Green as the main builder of the new harbour, and both he and his family were very prominent in public life in the town.

By 1811, the mouth of the Afon Aeron was a fairly disagreeable place. It was blocked by a shifting bar of stone and sand, which presented a formidable obstacle to any maritime traffic, and ships could be caught for weeks on end behind this bank near the river mouth. Despite this considerable impediment to trade, ships had been coming regularly to Aberaeron since the eighteenth century, and something had to be done. The lord of the manor, the Reverend Alban Thomas Jones Gwynne from Plas Tyglyn and, subsequently,

Mynachdy, was the pioneer. A document presented before Parliament in 1807 read as follows:

> The quay within the harbour of Aberaeron has become ruinous and insufficient for the Accommodation and Protection of the ships and vessels resorting to the said harbour. And whereas Alban Thomas Jones Gwynne, Clerk, Lord of the Manor . . . is willing and desirous at his own Expense to rebuild, enlarge, improve and maintain the said quay and pier and also to improve the said harbour.

The name of this great local benefactor has been immortalised in the name of the town's main square – Alban Square. The Reverend Gwynne was also keen to plan an attractive and well-appointed town, containing streets of tasteful houses built around the harbour and the main square. According to tradition, John Nash of Cardigan, one of the most renowned architects of the Georgian period, was responsible for the design of Aberaeron, but although Nash was friendly with the Gwynne family, it seems likely that it was not he but Edward Heycock of Shrewsbury who was the architect involved.

After the completion of the harbour walls and of the open but sheltered dock, Pwll Cam, which lay almost at the centre of the village, and of Doc Bach on its southern flank, which provided sheltered anchorage, Aberaeron developed rapidly. A fairly substantial woollen mill was established on the river bank, and nearby a forge was set up which became well known for the production of agricultural hand tools. The Aberaeron long-handled spade became famous throughout Britain and Ireland – particularly in the west and in Ireland – and many of the manufactured goods produced by these enterprises were exported from the harbour.

Although sailing ships went regularly from Aberaeron to Bristol and Liverpool – ships such as the *Andes* and the *Beryl* – from the earliest days of steam, from the 1860s onwards, Aberaeron acquired its own steamships. In 1863, the *Aberaeron Steam Navigation Company* was established with the *S.S. Prince Cadwgan*, which carried passengers and goods from the ports of western Wales to Liverpool, Bristol and occasionally to Ireland. In 1876 the *Prince Cadwgan* was lost near Solva in Pembrokeshire. A year later, in 1877, Thomas Davies established the *Aberayron Steam Packet Company*. The 87-ton *S.S. Ianthe* was acquired and sold in 1895 to a ship's master from Ayr in Scotland. In 1894, the company bought a larger vessel – the *Norseman*, a steamship of 194 tons, which was built in Paisley in Scotland in 1883. This ship continued sailing until 1918.

Strangely enough, the maritime trade continued longer in Aberaeron than almost any other port in Ceredigion. The main reason for this is that the railway was a comparative late-comer in reaching Aberaeron, and the town had to wait until 1911 before the railway from Lampeter went into daily use. A correspondent in 1902 remarked:

> Far removed from present day bustle and tumult, Aberaeron recalls an age before the transformation of the country by railways. It is only reached after a tedious journey by coach from Aberystwyth, Lampeter and Cardigan.

The railway did arrive, which put paid to the harbour as a trading centre.

As with New Quay to the south and Llanddewi Aber-arth to the north, the shipbuilding industry took on great importance at Aberaeron, particularly during the mid-nineteenth century. Before the harbour opened and shipbuilding became concentrated there, a few small vessels had been built locally, often on farms such as Cilfforch and Pengarreg, and even at the lonely cove at Gilfach yr Halen to the south of Aberaeron. Following the destruction in the big storm of 1844 of his important shipyard in Aber-arth, Evan Jones moved to the north side of Aberaeron harbour near the *Neptune* inn. There, he and his family were kept extremely busy until 1883, building a number of ships of all sizes. On the other side of the harbour, John Harris (Siôn Harri) and his family were equally busy constructing ships in the yard in front of his inn, the *Dolphin* (the *Dolphin* was subsequently named the *Trelawney*, and was home to the world famous opera singer, Sir Geraint Evans, until his death in the early 1990s). Some twenty-three ships were built in the yard at the *Dolphin*, and launched into the Doc Bach near the entrance to the harbour.

In 1841 there were ten individuals who described themselves as shipbuilders in Aberaeron; ten years later, the number had increased to twenty-three. There was fierce competition between Siôn Harri and his sons – John (Siôn Harri Bach), Henry and Dafydd – at the Dolphin yard, who built a total of twenty-three ships, and Evan Jones and his son Dafydd at the Neptune yard, particularly when it came to building the larger ships. In 1855, for example, Evan Jones built the 97-ton schooner, the *Gambia*. In the same year, Siôn Harri Bach launched the *William and Mary*, a brig of 239 tons from the Dolphin yard. In 1858, Evan Jones built the brig, *Xanthippe* (225 tons) and the schooner *Condor* (114 tons), while, in the following year, the Harris yard produced the *Leander* – a schooner of 72 tons – and the 143-ton brigantine, the *Maria Anna*.

As many as ninety-three ships were built at Aberaeron, the last of these being the ketch *Cadwgan* (123 tons), which is commemorated in the *Cadwgan* inn on the quay at Pwll Cam.

Despite the purchase by the *Aberayron Steam Packet Company* of the *S.S. Telephone* in 1910, specifically for voyages between Aberaeron and Liverpool, with the sale of the company in 1916 Aberaeron had reached the end of the line. Nevertheless, there was some hope of a revival in 1921, when a regular passenger service was started between Cardiff and Aberaeron by the Spillers company, who carried flour to Aberaeron. They used the small ships of Captains James and Davies from Llangrannog – ships such as the *Drumlough*, the *Enid Mary* and the *West Coaster*. An occasional cargo of stone or grit would arrive from Porth-gain and Trefor. In 1927, there were some twenty visits to the harbour, but by 1934 the last cargo of flour was landed by the *S.S. Drumlough*.

x)   Aber-arth

A little to the north of Aberaeron lies the small village of Llanddewi, located in a narrow valley at the point where the Afon Arth flows into the sea. The ancient church is hidden from the sea behind a hill, and this tiny settlement was once a hive of activity containing both a flour mill and an important woollen mill, which operated until the mid-twentieth century. There was also a major harbour here, in fact one of the oldest ports between Cardigan and Aberystwyth.

The main reason for such activity was its connection with the abbey at Strata Florida. For over three centuries, the monks of Strata Florida were an extremely influential power in Welsh life. Monks first came in 1164 to this remote area at the head of the Teifi valley, to establish a monastery that was far enough away from those influences which might have impinged on the strict rules of the Cistercian Order. In this inaccessible region, the White Monks built a huge abbey, which had an enormous influence on the Welsh economy until its dissolution in 1539. The work of building such a large establishment took fifty years to complete. For some reason, the monks were not willing to use local stone, and went to the trouble of importing stone from the Bristol area through the port of Llanddewi Aber-arth, and then transported it along difficult tracks to the lonely uplands some twenty miles away. Throughout the abbey's existence, Aber-arth served as its port and was also the site of several fisheries and weirs, which were developed to catch the abundance of fish in the bay. The remains of these weirs can be seen along the coast between Aberaeron and Aber-arth.

Aber-arth remained fairly busy as a port after the dissolution of the monasteries by Henry VIII. In addition to the port being a centre for the import of lime and fuel, it also developed shipbuilding. On the strip of land near the mouth of the Afon Arth, as many as twenty-five small ships were built – a small number compared with the ninety-three built at Aberaeron and the two hundred and forty in the New Quay area. Until the building of the port at Aberaeron in the second decade of the nineteenth century, Aber-arth was the more important site, and until 1844 Evan Jones and his company built ships here. Unfortunately, in 1844, there was a terrible storm, and a flood washed the contents of the Methodist chapel, including the communion table, out to sea. Evan Jones' shipyard was badly damaged and the 72-ton schooner the *Adroit* shared a similar fate to the chapel's communion table. The schooner was subsequently completed in Evan Jones' new yard on the north side of the harbour at Aberaeron. The big storm and flood was the death knell for activity in this ancient port at the mouth of the Afon Arth.

xi)   Llansanffraid

The villages of Llan-non and Llanrhystud on the main road from Aberystwyth to Aberaeron are quite a way from the sea, and between them and a township known as Traeth Llansanffraid, there is a flat piece of land which to this day is cultivated in long strips by a number of farms, just as was done in the Middle Ages. Despite their distance from the beach, Llan-non and Llanrhystud both have a long history of being homes to sailors. As in New Quay, Aberaeron and Llangrannog, the solid-looking and comparatively large houses that used to belong to sea captains can be seen scattered throughout these villages. Several of these dwellings bear the names of ships. For example, in the churchyard at Llansanffraid, there are impressive memorials to the people of the *Clarovina*, the *Ceylon*, the *Ontario*, the *Montrose*, the *Albion* and the *Turtle Dove*. In the same graveyard, a large number of sailors lie buried, or at least recorded on headstones, although Rangoon, Chile, Jamaica or Sydney may well have been their final resting place.

The beach at Llansanffraid developed as a fairly significant port during the nineteenth century, despite the fact that it lacks any real shelter. Like every other small port on the Ceredigion coast, lime, *cwlwm* and coal in particular were imported – the coal, from the Aberpergwm pit, was exported through Neath. At Craiglas, at the far end of the beach, there were some six limekilns and a wharf for the sloops that paid such frequent visits to the area. One of the earliest local ships was the *Spread Eagle*, which was owned by the Phillips family from New Quay – the family known as 'Y Cadnoed' [the Foxes]. In 1847, for example, the *Spread Eagle* brought a cargo of stout from the Guinness brewery in Dublin to the thriving *Felinfôr Brewery* on the coast at Llan-non. From there it went to Neath to collect *cwlwm* from the Aberpergwm pit, and then from southern Pembrokeshire it went to Craiglas with a cargo of lime.

Up until about 1865, the beach at Llansanffraid was extremely busy, and in addition to the small-scale import and export trade, shipbuilding also became very important here. Between 1824 and 1864, a total of some twenty-five ships were built. Between 1824 and 1845, Richard Williams built five ships and in 1830 John Evans built himself a ship, the *Enterprise*. Between 1856 and 1864 Daniel Evans built six ships, all of them substantial – brigs such as the *Egertere* (203 tons), and schooners such as the *Leander* (71 tons). During the same period – from around 1860 up until 1864 – Henry Harris, a member of the famous Harris family from Aberaeron, also built six ships: the barquentine *Aretas* (124 tons), the brigs *Convoy* (214 tons), the smack *Ann Eliza* (44 tons), the brigantine *Gwladys* (164 tons) and the schooner *Isabella* (69 tons), each one served by captains from Llan-non and Llanrhystud.

According to tradition, the Afon Wyre at Llanrhystud is the border between southern and northern Wales: the linguistic boundary between the use of the words 'nawr' and 'rŵan' in Welsh. Saint David never ventured further north than Llanrhystud.

6. CARDIGAN BAY – NORTH

i) Aberystwyth

Aberystwyth, the home of the National Library of Wales and the oldest college of the University of Wales, is the largest of the coastal towns in Cardigan Bay. This historic town was established by Edward I in the thirteenth century as a stronghold to protect his new regime from any Welsh insurgency in the area. On a hill above the mouth of the Afon Rheidol and the Afon Ystwyth, a major castle was built. This fortress was surrounded by marshy land, which provided a formidable defence against attacks from its hinterland, while the sea on its western side protected it from any assaults from that direction. In addition there was an extensive strand of gravel and mud – 'Y Ro Fawr' – which stretched south from the castle mound, and provided some sort of shelter for ships against the fury of the waves. Gradually a small town originally known as Llanbadarn Gaerog grew up around the castle. As a port it was not particularly prosperous. The bar across the estuary expanded rapidly, and it was necessary to wait for the winter storms and the flooding of the rivers to wash away some of the mud and sand that accumulated around Y Ro Fawr. The impact of this bar on the development of Aberystwyth as a port was such that in 1561 Aberystwyth was described as 'a barred haven of no value' and this state of affairs prevailed until the beginning of the eighteenth century. Since Cromwell's army had inflicted considerable damage on the castle, a number of the town's inhabitants had been in too run-down and dismal a condition to deal with herring fishing. But by 1755 Aberystwyth had a fleet of some sixty fishing boats. Each boat had a crew of seven who fished the most abundant fisheries that

Cardigan Bay has ever seen. Herring fishing was an autumn and winter occupation. One observer notes:

> Here was an industry which could have brought wealth to the town, but there was no one prepared to do the necessary organising. In 1702, 1734 barrels of fish were sent to Ireland in English or Irish ships. By the middle of the century, the trade was almost entirely in the hands of merchants from Liverpool whose practice it was to send ships from the Isle of Man to Aberystwyth then to purchase and salt fish ready for export.

Slowly but surely during the course of the eighteenth century, the herring market deteriorated, particularly because the herring stocks had been seriously depleted, and in 1744 it was reported that 'the herring that occurred so profusely [is now] a stranger to the coast'. Meanwhile, it was Aberdyfi and not Aberystwyth that was considered to be the main port in the north of Cardigan Bay, and it was also the registry for the region, much to the chagrin of the fishermen and traders of Aberystwyth. After all, Aberdyfi comprised no more than a handful of cottages. In 1763, the people of Aberystwyth managed to move the shipping registry to Aberystwyth – to Stryd y Tollty (Custom House Street). The fishermen of Aberystwyth would sail along the coast in the spring and summer, during the months when they were not fishing for herring, shipping out goods such as oak bark for the leather industry and a certain amount of lead ore. They would also import lime, coal and, of course, large quantities of salt for the fishing industry.

Ships that came to Aberystwyth were faced with tremendous problems, and it soon became clear that there would have to be investment in a new harbour if there was to be any sort of commercial growth. In 1780, legislation was passed to commence work on improving the harbour. However, the Harbour Trustees were very reluctant to spend any large sums of money. Unfortunately, the new harbourmaster, William Jolson, disappeared with a considerable amount of the trustees' funds. During the final decade of the eighteenth century, there was rapid expansion in the lead mining industry, and all sorts of goods were now imported to Aberystwyth, which was itself expanding apace. In 1792 Aberystwyth had some ninety ships on its register. Despite all obstacles, shipbuilding had become a major industry at the port. There was a regular service by sea to Bristol and Liverpool, and the need to improve the harbour became even more apparent. In 1836 a new scheme was commenced, which was far more ambitious than any of the cheap, short-term plans that had been the hallmark of the schemes promulgated by Aberystwyth traders in previous years. The course of both the Ystwyth and the Rheidol were now altered so that the rivers would be able to scour out the harbour. In addition, a carved stone pier about 210 yards long was built on the landward side of Y Ro Fawr. The Ro Fawr was strengthened with a network of groynes and, with another pier, which was built on the southern side, the sheltered harbour was complete and was able to receive quite large vessels. With the building of a number of warehouses along the quayside, Aberystwyth developed into a major port. The process of building and the construction of the harbour foundations was very slow, and stone from the Allt-wen quarry near Tan-y-bwlch beach was used for the work. To carry the stone to the harbour, a narrow-gauge railway was built from the quarry.

After the construction of strong walls around the harbour, in the 1840s Aberystwyth began to flourish, becoming a port of registration in 1847, responsible for all the landing-places and beaches in Cardigan Bay from New Quay in the south to Tywyn in the north. This was completely at odds with the wishes of the people of Cardigan in the south, and Aberdyfi in the north. By 1850, Aberystwyth was responsible for two hundred and thirteen ships, comprising a total of 12,458 tons, which were registered in Aberystwyth. In 1853, an insurance company, *The Aberystwyth Mutual Ship Insurance Company*, was set up, and took its place alongside similar companies in Aber-porth, New Quay and Aberaeron, which no longer had to depend on London-based companies to underwrite local ships.

Until 1882, when the last of Aberystwyth's ships was launched – the 95-ton schooner, the *Edith Eleanor* – the town had been renowned as a shipbuilding centre and a total of two hundred and twenty-four ships were built in Aberystwyth yards. Many of these – from the smallest smack, such as the *Urgent* (13 tons), right up to the largest brigantine such as the *Rachel Lewis* (242 tons) – were the work of three generations of the Evans family: Faulk Evans, his son John and his grandson John Faulk Evans. Around the harbour were located the workshops of all the craftsmen required in the shipbuilding industry – premises for the ropemakers and sailmakers as well as metal foundries and pulley block workshops.

Aberystwyth was now importing all manner of goods – lime and *cwlwm* from southern Wales, stout from Dublin, and timber from Scandinavia, the Baltic and even from ports such as Quebec, Dalhousie, Three Rivers and Miramichi in north America. In time, as happened in New Quay, it was cheap, inferior vessels that dealt a blow to Aberystwyth shipbuilding, a blow from which it would never recover.

The export of lead ore from the rich mines of north-west Ceredigion was vital to the port. From the remote hillsides came lead and zinc for export to the refineries in Bristol, Swansea and the ports of the Afon Dee, but with the arrival of the railway from Shrewsbury in 1864 and another from Carmarthen in 1867, the maritime trade of the town declined, and despite the opening of a narrow-gauge line to Pont-ar-fynach in 1902, which was supposed to give a boost to the lead industry, the industry did not in fact have much of a future. By 1939 there was very little sea traffic passing through Aberystwyth, and tourism became the mainstay of the town which, for a few years, had seen so much activity.

In addition to the hustle and bustle of the export and import trade, Aberystwyth, particularly in the days before the railway, was also busy running regular services to Liverpool and Bristol, with companies such as *The Aberystwyth and Aberdovey Steam Packet Company* sailing almost every week. For example, the *Countess of Lisburne* would sail to Bristol, charging her passengers the following rates:

Cabin 5/-
Return 7/6
Fore Deck 3/-
Return 4/6

There were also occasional passages for emigrants, such as on the *Credo* in the 1840s. One of the small shipowners of Aberystwyth – John Mathias, a grocer from 7 Heol y Bont – earned his fame and fortune as a Cardiff shipowner. In 1876 he had two sailing ships, the *Miss Evans* and the *Solway*, which brought goods from Liverpool and Bristol to his shop in Aber. In 1883 the *Glanrheidol Steamship Company* was established, and acquired the steamship *Glanrheidol*, which weighed 1005 tons and was much too big to sail from Aberystwyth. The main work of the *Glanrheidol* and the five other vessels purchased by the company was the carrying of coal from Cardiff. As mentioned earlier, John Mathias was an elder in Y Tabernacl, the Presbyterian chapel, and he persuaded several of his fellow elders, members of the congregation and even the minister himself, the Rev. Thomas Levi, to invest heavily in his venture. Another of his financial backers was Thomas Charles Edwards, the first principal of the college in Aberystwyth.

In October 1896, the *Cambrian Steam Navigation Company* was established. By this time Richard Mathias, the second son of John Mathias, was running the company's second office in Cardiff, as well as the Aberystwyth office. Why a shipowner from Aberystwyth decided to name his ships after English public schools nobody knows, but before too long the company became known as the College Line, with ships such as the *Harrovian, Etonian, Rugbeian* and the *Breconian* replacing the *Glanystwyth*, the *Glanhafren* and others, all built by the William Doxford works in Sunderland. By 1906 the College Line had eight steamships in excess of 3000 tons sailing worldwide, especially from the coal ports of southern Wales to the Mediterranean and the Black Sea. To the business community in Cardiff, 'Aberystwyth ships' meant the fleet belonging to John Mathias and his son, and people from Aberystwyth and Y Borth comprised a great number of the officers and captains of their vessels. After the death of John Mathias in 1912 he was succeeded by his son, (Sir) Richard Mathias, who ran the company until 1922.

ii)   Y Borth and Ynys-las

Nowadays, Y Borth is a long ribbon development of houses between the sea and Cors Fochno – a holiday village containing a large number of second homes. There is an older settlement here – that of Aberleri to the south of the ancient bogland of Cors Fochno. To the east, the valley of the Afon Leri was a centre for important industries, its waters powering several flour mills and at least six woollen mills. An historian in 1903 observed:

> The older part of the town is quaintly irregular and the promenade here gives place to a street of varying width the houses on the seaward side facing the road and not the sea, so that from the sands the houses present a ruinous jumble of back premises and wooden boundaries.

The inhabitants of the old village of Aberleri were undoubtedly fishermen. The most significant development in the area was the arrival of the *Aberystwyth and Welsh Coast Railway* in 1863-64. It destroyed local maritime trade almost immediately, and the last sloop, the *Prosperity*, left in 1863. In addition, the Afon Leri was redirected in 1901 to run straight into the Dyfi, as part of an ambitious scheme to drain the Fochno bog. Apart from families such as the Bells, who ran the ferry service from Ynys-las to Aberdyfi, tourism was the main industry in the Borth area. Only in one place, near Ynys-las, where the Leri now flows into the Dyfi, is there a shipyard that is still in operation, which specialises in steel fishing boats. Between 1842 and 1851, some eight sloops were built here for use by local sailors. Two other ships were built in the old part of Y Borth: the 79-ton schooner the *Catherine and Ellen* in 1842, and a smack called the *Lerry* in 1871.

iii)   Aberdyfi and Derwen-las

Aberdyfi is by now a seaside resort whose energies are all directed to serving the tourist industry. It contains numerous hotels and restaurants, accommodation for visitors, and second homes for city dwellers. With a golf course, and moorings for pleasure craft of all sizes, present-day activity is very different from what it used to be. At one time Aberdyfi was a lively and bustling port that exported slate and lead, and for a short time it was a centre for shipbuilding. These days you hardly hear any Welsh in Aberdyfi and the accents of the English Midlands now prevail in every pub and shop. The link between this town and the Midlands is not a new departure. After all, this is the nearest place that people from Birmingham and Wolverhampton can go to get some sea air. In fact, according to the local business community in 1880, one of the great advantages of Aberdyfi was its convenient location in relation to the Midlands. It was in that year that the *Waterford and Aberdovey Steamship Company* was established, with the intention of providing a regular service between the Midlands and Ireland. There were even dreams of running a service from the mouth of the Dyfi to New York. The advent of the railway in 1867 had dealt a mortal blow to the shipyard at Penhelig, the village that lay at the mouth of the Dyfi. However, all was not lost. D.W. Morgan observed in 1948:

> Many were thinking that this town would be broken up after the coming of the railway but now it is not the case. Trade is increasing and will continue to do so.

With the construction of new wharves and warehouses on the shore in 1882 and the building of a jetty stretching out into the river, Aberdyfi had every appearance of being an important port. In order to boost the import of timber, corn, fuel and goods of all sorts, and the export of Corris slates and agricultural produce, the wharves were linked to a network of railways. In the port itself there were livestock pens to hold sheep, cattle and pigs that were imported from Ireland and England, before they were loaded into railway trucks to be despatched all over the country.

As far back as the seventeenth century, Penhelyg already identified as such – was extremely busy as a major herring port, and was in fierce competition with Aberystwyth to the south. Rivalry over their status was a hard-fought battle between the two ports, and it was a matter of concern to the inhabitants of Aberdyfi when they lost the right to register ships in 1847, and Aberystwyth was made responsible for all the ports from New Quay in the south to the mouth of the Afon Dysynni in the north.

As well as the jealousy that existed between Aberdyfi and Aberystwyth, there was a considerable degree of animosity between the inhabitants and merchants of Aberdyfi and those of Barmouth to the north. Both places had their sights on becoming the main port for Meirionnydd. Barmouth was already an important harbour, and the shipbuilding industry along the Afon Mawddach was particularly renowned. A number of shipbuilders from the Afon Mawddach were persuaded to move to the Aberdyfi area to work at the Penhelyg shipyards. The main type of ship to be built at Aberdyfi was the schooner, particularly after 1840. According to D.W. Morgan in his volume *Brief Glory*, as many as fifty-five schooners were built on the banks of the Dyfi, in locations such as Aberdyfi, Penhelyg, Aberleri, Morben and Derwen-las. In addition a barque, two brigantines, three brigs and fourteen sloops were also built.

The beach at Aberdyfi was the workplace of shipbuilders such as the eccentric Roger Lewis, who built brigantines and sloops that tended to capsize in stormy weather, and John Jones (Jac y Traeth) who was considered to be something of a genius. The greatest of them all was Thomas Richards, who built fourteen ships on a piece of land that is now a public park in the middle of Aberdyfi.

In the final quarter of the nineteenth century, the shipbuilding industry on the banks of the Afon Dyfi came to an end, having been destroyed by the big ships of Canada and north-east England.

Up until about the mid-nineteenth century, Derwen-las, some two miles from Machynlleth, was an extremely busy harbour – in fact this was Montgomeryshire's only port. It was mostly Corris slate that was exported from here and a tramway was built from Corris to the river port at Derwen-las. Lead ore, much of it from the remote mines of Dylife was also exported, carried to the village by means of horse and cart. Oak bark and timber, flannel and a variety of country produce and goods were exported from Derwen-las, and although the ambitious plan to cut a canal from Derwen-las to Machynlleth never materialised, the little harbour was essential to the area. One observer stated in 1852:

> The river Dovey is navigable to Derwen-las and affords a facility of conveying the produce of the quarries and mines to their destination and of supplying the neighbourhood with various commodities. The average annual exports from the place are 500 tons of bark; 40,000 feet of oak timber; 150,000 yards of oak pole for collieries, 100 tons of lead ore and 1500 tons of slate. The average annual imports are 5000 quarters of rye and wheat, 1000

tons of coal, 500 tons of culm, 2000 tons of limestone, 11,000 English and foreign hides and groceries and other shop goods to the amount of £14,000 in value.

This indicates that Derwen-las was clearly a fairly prosperous river port of great value to the inhabitants of the Dyfi valley and of Montgomeryshire. As usual such commercial importance led to the development of shipbuilding, particularly downriver at Morben Isaf (which is now a caravan park). Rowland Evans and his family, who were from Dinas Mawddwy, settled in Morben in 1845. A fervent Congregationalist, he began building ships at Morben, the first of which was the 76-ton schooner, the *Sarah and Mary*. This was followed by a number of others, such as the smack *Seven Brothers* (46 tons) and the schooner *Miss Evans* (97 tons) in 1855. As well as building high quality schooners, the Evans family were also good sailors. Other schooners were built, such as the *Deborah* and the *Idris*, as well as a smack, the *Morben*, all of which sailed in the name of the Evans family of Morben Isaf, Derwen-las. By the 1860s, there was trouble ahead as the railway was extended from Machynlleth to Aberystwyth. This was not only to have a detrimental effect on the port at Derwen-las but also, with the construction of a large railway bridge near Glandyfi and Dyfi Junction, was to make any upstream traffic impossible. The history of Montgomeryshire's only port came to an end with the building in 1869 of the last of its ships – the *Catherine* of 70 tons.

By 1870, the busy maritime trade on the banks of the Afon Dyfi had decreased enormously. The railway, which had initially been seen as saving the fortunes of the river and its harbour, soon replaced the maritime trade. Lead mining came to an end in the hills of Montgomeryshire; the all-important slate industry at

Corris, Aberllefenni and many other places waned, and the wool trade, which at one time had held sway in Machynlleth and southern Meirionnydd, also came to an end. Although all types of timber were still imported, and although the huge Melin Ardudwy factory would keep going for some time to come, by 1914 the era of commercial prosperity was over, and only the tourists were left.

iv)   Barmouth

Although the mouth of the Afon Dysynni near Tywyn saw a certain amount of activity, in the form of the landing of some essential commodities for the local community, and the building of two or three small ships, no real port developed between the Afon Dyfi and Mawddach. Barmouth, and places such as Llyn Penmaen and Maes-y-garnedd in the Dolgellau area were once hives of activity, with large-scale shipbuilding taking place on the banks of the Afon Mawddach. Between 1750 and 1865, as many as three hundred and eighteen ships were built at Barmouth, the product of three shipyards in the town. For some years, despite competition from the traders of Aberdyfi, Barmouth was Meirionnydd's main port. Nowadays, there is little to show that this ancient town was one of the important ports of Wales, with world-wide connections.

In addition to the immense amount of trade that took place in Barmouth during the eighteenth century, the town, with its narrow streets squeezed between the steep cliffs and the long sandy beach, was one of the earliest centres for the tourist trade. The Cors-y-Gedol hotel, with its 'warm seawater baths', was built as early as 1795, and when the poet William Wordsworth came to Barmouth on holiday in 1823, and again in 1825, he was full of praise:

> I took a boat and rowed up its sublime estuary which may be compared with the finest in Scotland. With a fine sea view in front, the mountains behind, the glorious estuary running eight miles inland and Cader Idris within the compass of a day's walk, Barmouth can hold its own against any rival.

Another poet, Alfred Lord Tennyson, although not particularly complimentary with regard to the virtues of Barmouth, could at least acknowledge that 'Barmouth is a great deal prettier than Aberystwyth'. Barmouth's popularity as a holiday centre continued, as did its status as Meirionnydd's main port until about the mid-nineteenth century. Today, the port itself is fairly insignificant, with no more than a few fishing boats and pleasure craft. For many, this old town manifests all the worst aspects of tourism, containing as it does all the tasteless attractions of a fun-fair and night clubs, fast-food outlets and tacky shops. With all its tall, fine houses converted into flats as housing for the homeless from English cities, Barmouth today is hardly recognisable as the town which at one time would attract thousands, including such eminent visitors as Charles Darwin and William Gladstone.

One of the main reasons for Barmouth becoming one of the main ports in northern Wales was the development of the woollen industry, particularly during the eighteenth century. This was the most important of Meirionnydd's industries at the time, and the weavers who worked at home or in the factories were fundamental to the county's economy. The centre of this activity was at Dolgellau, but the industry was evident in every valley and village and, up until about 1770, the product of the looms would be taken to

Shrewsbury to be sold at the weekly market, which was owned by a fairly unprincipled cartel of merchants – the *Shrewsbury Drapers' Company*. In 1770 the monopoly of this English company was broken, and in 1772 a depot and warehouse were set up in Barmouth to serve as a collection point for local woollen cloth for export to many parts of the world – to Europe, north America and Mexico. It is said that in 1790 as many as 276,612 yards of cloth were sent from Barmouth, but with the onset of the Napoleonic Wars the export trade came to an end in 1796. It was revived on a much smaller scale after 1815. In the history of the Welsh woollen industry, flannels from Meirionnydd, known as 'webs', were considered the roughest of materials and the main market for such cloth was for slaves in America. The market continued up until the 1860s when slavery was abolished. Until that time ships from Barmouth would sail on a regular basis across the Atlantic to ports such as Charleston and New Orleans, which were slavery centres.

Although a large number of commodities were imported to Barmouth, it developed principally as a shipbuilding centre, and at the end of the eighteenth century and beginning of the nineteenth, the banks of the Afon Mawddach, along with Pwllheli, were the main producers of ships of all sizes in northern Wales. As long as the woollen industry was in good shape there was a demand for ships – particularly for square-rigged brigs – that could easily make the passage across the Atlantic. After 1820 a number of schooners were built, but during this period Pwllheli was more important as a shipbuilding centre. The shipbuilding industry on the Afon Mawddach ended with the construction of the schooner *Glynn* in 1865, and Porthmadog and Borth-y-gest developed as new centres.

As well as three shipyards in Barmouth, there was also shipbuilding in many places along the river almost as far upstream as Llanelltyd and Dolgellau. In 1798, for example, the conditions at Llyn Penmaen are described as follows:

> At this place the tide flows to a considerable height and a number of small craft with a few large vessels are built. A brig of about 200 tons was now upon the stocks and others of inferior size, but vessels of any considerable tonnage are obliged to be launched about the equinoxes, to take advantage of the high vernal and autumnal tides for floating over the bar at Barmouth.

With the arrival of the railway in the 1860s, trade came to an end and Meirionnydd's leading port went into terminal decline. As Aled Eames observes:

> One is very much aware of the host of seamen who ventured forth from the mouth of the Afon Mawddach to distant parts of the world. Among them were many colourful characters, such as Captain William Timothy (1760-1833), who sailed on a regular basis from Liverpool to St Petersburg on his ship, the *Felicity*, which was built on the banks of the Afon Mawddach in 1805; Captain Dedwydd, and the first Captain Griffith, both from Pembrokeshire, and the renowned Captain Griffith E. Dedwydd (Dedwith), who was master of several of Porthmadog's famous schooners; and Captain Richard who became one of the leading captains of the *Black Ball Line*, and who was the son of a shipwright from Barmouth.

v)   Porthmadog

As a major port from the beginning of the nineteenth century, Porthmadog relied entirely on the wealth quarried from the mountains which surrounded it. It was the port for the all-important slate industry of Blaenau Ffestiniog, and became one of the main ports of Wales – both as a trading centre and for building some of the most graceful and beautiful sailing ships the world has ever seen. These were described as Western Ocean Yachts, which came into existence in the twilight years when steamships had begun to replace sailing ships on the ocean. Here, in a remote corner of Cardigan Bay, the shipbuilders of Porthmadog and Borth-y-gest built some of the most majestic craft ever to sail. Between about 1891 and 1913, the schooners built here represented a high point in the craft of shipbuilding. Over two hundred sailing vessels were built at Porthmadog. The main work undertaken by these schooners was the export of slates from Ffestiniog and service to the fishing trade of Newfoundland and Labrador. Salt from different parts of Europe was shipped to distant ports in Canada, such as Venison Tickle and Peggy's Bay, which were important centres for the salting and drying of cod. The fish would then be exported to ports in the Mediterranean, such as Genoa, Gibraltar, Naples and Leghorn. The Western Ocean Yachts weighed less than two hundred tons because under the regulations of the Merchant Shipping Acts, the use of larger ships would mean having to carry a licensed mate. With a crew of seven or eight, Porthmadog ships such as the *Blodwen* (the first) and the *Gestiana* (the last, lost on her maiden voyage between Newfoundland and Cape Breton Island in 1913) were designed and built specifically for the fishing trade. This was the last remaining trade in which it was more profitable to utilise sail than steam, and the beautiful schooners built by David Jones, David Williams and Ebenezer Morris were superlative examples of the craft of building wooden sailing ships. The industry continued to prosper up until the beginning of the First World War. Basil Greenhill observed:

> It was in the Newfoundland trade that the British Schooner was developed to its highest form in the shipyards of Porthmadog . . . This development occurred between 1891 when the Blodwen was launched and 1913 when the last of the Porthmadog schooners was built. The vessels were three masted schooners of very similar size and similar shape, a conscious attempt by Porthmadog shipbuilders and owners to design and produce an ideal small merchant sailing ship to trade continuously under all conditions on deep water.

Of course, for years prior to the days of building the *Blodwen*, the first Western Ocean Yacht, Porthmadog had been renowned for the export of slates throughout the world. 'The Port' would never have developed as it did, if it had not been for the actions of one person, William Alexander Maddocks, who built the town of Tremadog and the long seawall – the Cob – in order to reclaim two thousand acres of sea marsh at the mouth of the Afon Glaslyn. By 1825, Porthmadog was very much on the map and was already exporting slates from Blaenau. Shipbuilding took off at an early date, Henry Jones launching the 65-ton schooner the *Two Brothers* from Traeth Mawr (or Canol y Clwt) in June 1824. This ship belonged to her master, William Parry, a slate loader called Daniel Hughes, and a local farmer, Daniel Parry. This was the first of two hundred and fifty-six ships to be built there. Between 1824 and 1860 at this spot, which later became known as Greaves Wharf, Henry Jones built as many as thirty sloops, barques and schooners especially for the slate trade.

Despite all appearances, Porthmadog was difficult to access: mariners had to exercise extreme caution in crossing the bar near Ynys Cyngar and sailing along the narrow channel as far as Porthmadog itself. There were also considerable dangers lurking in the bay, with such nautical hazards as Sarn Badrig and Porth Neigwl causing the destruction of many ships. Through the strenuous efforts of W.A. Madocks and his company, things were looking up, and by 1824 the new harbour was vastly improved. The owners of the Blaenau Ffestiniog quarries were busy building their own wharfs – Samuel Holland from Rhiwbryfdir was the first, closely followed by John Whitehead Greaves of Llechwedd quarry and, finally, by the eponymous owner of the Oakley quarry, the biggest of them all. The town sprang up rapidly around the harbour, a town whose whole existence was focused on the sea and its traffic. There were nautical schools and ship insurance companies as well as different craftsmen to meet the requirements of the maritime trade. Aled Eames states:

> Porthmadog was the busiest port for sailing ships in Cardigan Bay . . . According to *Pilot* 1902, some five hundred ships entered Porthmadog every year, bringing in coal, lime, and timber from America and Scandinavia, and of course, shipping out slates. The demand for Ffestiniog slates in Hamburg and Stettin continued up to 1914, and some buildings in Germany are still roofed with Welsh slate, despite the ravages of two world wars.

Had it not been for the wealth in the hills around Blaenau Ffestiniog, it seems unlikely that Porthmadog would have developed at all. One of the major disadvantages of Ffestiniog was the difficulty of exporting the slates from this mountainous parish – the town does not lie on the shores of a major waterway. However the Afon Glaslyn and the Dwyryd, which were situated a few miles away, were vital for the carriage of slate. The Afon Dwyryd is almost six miles in length and although it begins its course at breakneck speed, it also slows suddenly, opening out into a truly magnificent and expansive estuary leading to the sea. Wooded mountain slopes look down on extensive stretches of meadowland, in stark contrast to the grey and rather foreboding landscape around Blaenau. It was here that a number of the local quarry owners decided to build their grand residences, and several early quays were built along the riverbank in the vicinity of Maentwrog and Tan-y-bwlch. Before the construction of the Ffestiniog narrow-gauge railway in 1836, the slates were taken by horseback or in carts and wagons, and were loaded onto boats that sailed regularly up and down the river, from which their cargoes were transferred to larger ships waiting in a fairly unsuitable anchorage at Ynys Cyngar.

The men who worked on the slate boats were rough and violent. They wore high hard hats and plus-fours and were known as the Philistines. The wooden boats, carrying up to 8 tons of slate, each had a crew of two – the master and a boy to assist him. It is said that as many as forty boats – such as the *Mackerel*, the *Wenci*, the *Cwch Coch*, the *Gwalch* and others – sailed the Afon Glaslyn to Ynys Cyngar. All the wharves also had their own names, and were built to meet the needs of the various Blaenau slate owners. Between Maentwrog and the sea there were, for example, Cemlyn Quay, Paris Quay, Felenrhyd, Pen Trwyn y Garnedd, Brynmawr, Tyddyn Isa and Gelli Grin.

After the building of the narrow-gauge railway from

Blaenau Ffestiniog to the sea in 1837, the days of the Philistines came to an end, although one or two endeavoured to carry on working up until about 1860.

vi)   Pwllheli and Cricieth

Modern-day Pwllheli is a busy place, a haven for hundreds of pleasure boats in a magnificent marina, and a holiday resort for thousands. The port also has a long history involving a very different type of maritime trade. Despite providing unsatisfactory shelter from ocean gales, at Pwllheli one of the most important shipbuilding centres of northern Wales developed. Between 1782 and 1878 as many as four hundred and twenty-one ships were built there, varying in size from little 7-ton or 8-ton sloops to the huge 693-ton *Margaret Pugh*, which was intended for world-wide trading. It is ironic that in a town where the Calvinistic Methodist denomination held sway, a number of ships in Pwllheli were built for the slave trade. A visitor in 1801 observed:

> This little town seems in a flourishing condition. I saw a large Guineman on the stocks, fitted for 600 slaves.

It was a further coincidence that this ship, which was destined to trade between Liverpool, west Africa and America, was being built at the same time as the nearby Penmount Methodist chapel. In fact, three of the elders of that chapel, Hugh Pugh and John and Owen Edwards, were the main owners of the *Margaret Pugh*, the largest of Pwllheli's ships.

Pwllheli's development into a shipbuilding centre is quite surprising. There was very little oak suitable for building wooden ships available in Llŷn, and from the earliest days at the end of the eighteenth century, timber for building had to be imported from other countries. Oak was imported from the areas around Barmouth and Aberdyfi and by the late eighteenth century, timber ships from Aberystwyth, Liverpool and Cardiff were regular visitors to Pwllheli. The timber merchants at the port, who were also involved with shipbuilding, soon realised that it was cheaper for them to import timber – particularly pinewood and softwoods – from Scandinavia, the Baltic and north America. In the 1830s, for example, William Hughes and Lewis Evans, both shopkeepers in the town, established two timber yards. Nearby, William Jones, the druggist, set up a shipyard and built a number of small sloops for the coastal trade, upgrading to build the somewhat larger *Ann*, which was intended to carry cargoes of timber from Quebec to Pwllheli. William Jones became an important businessman because as well as building ships he was also the owner of a large timber yard and one of the founders of the Pwllheli brewery. William Jones of Brynhyfryd and Robert Evans of Cadlys built a number of ships for their own use and also for the traders of Liverpool, some of whom had been born in Pwllheli. The town grew in importance, and became known as the 'Welsh Emporium for Shipbuilding'. In the 1840s, there could be as many as twenty-eight ships on the stocks at the same time. It is also said that there could be as many as twenty-eight shipwrights working on a single vessel at any given time, and there were also blacksmiths, and makers of sails, pulley-blocks and ropes in regular employment. According to the 1841 census, in a town of two thousand six hundred inhabitants there were thirty-nine shipwrights, five shipbuilders, nine sawyers, one pulley-block maker, three ropemakers, seven painters and seven blacksmiths. In addition, the yards attracted craftsmen from other areas.

As the years went by, the builders of Pwllheli were able to meet the demands coming from Porthmadog for schooners in particular to export Blaenau Ffestiniog slate all over the world, but before too long, following the huge development in shipbuilding at Porthmadog and Borth-y-gest, there was less demand for the services of the Pwllheli builders. With the development of iron ships and steam, Pwllheli's days as the Ship Emporium came to an end.

Despite the dangers of Traeth Neigwl and the dreadful Atlantic storms, Llŷn depended to a large extent on the trade of its fishermen and sailors, but Pwllheli was the only port of any consequence in the area. Early in the nineteenth century, a number of businessmen – Philip Constable from Northampton, John Holland from Brentford and Gilbert Fairlie from Watford – came to Pwllheli to build a quay and warehouses in the town. The town afforded a bit more shelter from the prevailing winds than the old quay at Traeth Tŷ-Iddew [Jew's House Beach]. It was the hope of these early in-migrants – as was the case with Sol Andrews from Cardiff, who invested in Pwllheli in the early twentieth century – that they would reap great rewards from their investment in this isolated corner of north-west Wales. With shipbuilding and the output from local slate and granite quarries, Pwllheli was busy enough, but by the last quarter of the nineteenth century, trade was declining extremely rapidly. In an attempt to stop the decline, a new quay called Tugela Wharf was built at Pen-y-cob, but every effort to revive trade was in vain – the good times were over.

Although the beach at Cricieth, in the shelter of the castle, saw a fair bit of maritime activity, it cannot be compared to the bustle of Porthmadog and Borth-y-gest to the east, or Pwllheli to the west. All kinds of goods would be landed on the beach, from fuel to manure, from groceries to crockery. As in all the other coastal towns and villages in Gwynedd, seamanship was an integral part of life in Cricieth, with a large proportion of the town's young men becoming seamen. Many of Cricieth's businessmen realised their ambitions as shipowners in Liverpool. For example, Robert Thomas, a former schoolteacher, established a company in Liverpool and by 1895 owned fourteen large ships. With offices in Cricieth and in Richmond Buildings, Liverpool, Robert Thomas was not only keen to appoint captains and crews from his home locality, but he was also keen to attract capital from Cricieth and Pwllheli. The company was extremely successful, and between 1878 and 1913 had as many as thirty-eight large ships, most of them manufactured by William Doxford from Sunderland. Many of these ships had Welsh names, such as the *Ednyfed, Gwynedd, Maelgwyn* and the *Cadwgan*, and, of course, the *Criccieth Castle*.

vii)   Aberdaron and Pen Draw Llŷn

Nowhere in Llŷn is very far from the sea, and over the centuries the region's inhabitants depended on fishing for all types of fish, and on small coastal ships. During the summer months, a fair amount of activity would come to the beaches at Aberdaron, Porth Sgadan, Porth Gwylan, Porth Golmon, Porth Tŷ Mawr, Porth Ferin, Porth Iago, Porthoer and Porth y Wrach, where small ships, some of them belonging to local people, landed countless goods. The majority of these small ships came from ports such as Liverpool and Caernarfon, since there was very little traffic between the farthest reaches of Llŷn and the north of Cardigan Bay.

The rocky coastline and wild seas, with the

incredible tidal race sweeping through Bardsey Sound, make this a particularly difficult region for small ships, and yet it was this type of vessel that provided the link between the wider world and this isolated peninsula. The majority of the ports in Llŷn, with the exception of Aberdaron and Abersoch, are located on the more sheltered northern coast. Some beaches served a single farmstead, and as well as importing the essentials of fuel, lime, crockery and food, they would export casks of butter, salt fish, eggs and poultry for distant markets. A number of the small ships – sloops and ketches – were frequent and regular visitors to Llŷn. For example, during the summers of 1916 and 1917, the *Tryfan* visited Porth Golmon a total of ten times. According to Sir Thomas Parry, between 1910 and 1914 the *Tryfan* and the *Colonel Gamble* would call at Liverpool, Runcorn, Widnes, Holyhead, Cemaes, Moelfre, Beaumaris, Menai Bridge, Y Felinheli, Porth Dinllaen, Porth Sgadan, Porth Golmon and Abersoch. The *Colonel Gamble* was a small 60-ton ketch, and it was lost on the rugged rocks of Porth Golmon in November 1913.

The coastal trade continued for a long time after the end of the First World War. In fact, in a region that was never served by the railways or suitable roads, the coastal trade probably lasted longer in Llŷn than in any other area of Wales.

Over the centuries, Aberdaron was of course the main port for Bardsey Island, and in the days when there was a sizeable population on the island, the link between Bardsey and the mainland was extremely important. In 1881, for example, the island had a population of a hundred and thirty-two individuals, who were entirely dependent on small ships regularly delivering all kinds of goods. The trade in the produce of Bardsey, especially livestock and fish – shellfish such as crab and lobster in particular – relied entirely on ships and seamanship to reach the market. In his account of travels in northern Wales in 1800, William Bingley observes: 'Collecting of lobsters and crabs occupied most of the time of the inhabitants of Bardsey and the catch was sent to Liverpool by boat'. From Bingley's time early in the nineteenth century until 1914, these ships were an essential part of the island's economy and the islanders' way of life.

In the nineteenth century, a certain amount of boatbuilding took place in Pen Llŷn. Most of the work done by local builders involved the building of fishing boats. These had to be both strong and broad in the beam in order to withstand the storms and dangerous currents in this part of Wales. Early in the twentieth century, there were boat yards at Aberdaron, Abersoch, Llanbedrog and Porth Golmon. The most famous of the builders was John Thomas, a native of Bardsey, who built boats at his workshop in Y Rhiw until his death in around 1965. Llŷn boats – or *cychod Enlli* as they were called – were usually some twelve to sixteen feet in length, and some four and half feet across, with sufficient depth and strength to withstand high seas. There was a difference between *cychod banw*, 'female boats' which had two sails – a mainsail and a jib – and four oars, and *cychod gwrw*, 'male boats'. These were much smaller craft, designed to be rowed with four heavy oars, rather than being put under sail. Larch was the usual timber used to build the unique boats of Llŷn.

7.   CAERNARFON BAY AND THE MENAI STRAIT

i)   Nefyn and Porth Dinllaen

The maritime tradition on the northern coast of Llŷn was very strong, and villages such as Nefyn and Porth Dinllaen on the shores of their sheltered bay were particularly significant. Both Trefor and Nant Gwrtheyrn at the foot of Yr Eifl also became busy ports for the export of granite to other parts of the country, while villages such as Tudweiliog and Edern, which were some distance from the coast, also had a strong maritime tradition. Of course, the coast of northern Llŷn was somewhat more sheltered than the southern coast, and in the bay at Porth Dinllaen, protected by Morfa Nefyn and the mountains of Yr Eifl, trade developed greatly. Some one hundred and twenty-five ships were built there between 1760 and 1880. The last to be built was the 120-ton schooner *Venus*, which was built on the seashore at Griffith Owen's yard. Nefyn ships were considered to be extremely robust and able to sail the roughest sea. Some of them, such as the 190-ton barquentine *Linus*, would sail regularly round the Horn to Chile and Peru. One of the largest to be built at Nefyn was the 287-ton barque, the *Robert Jones*, built in 1866 and eventually wrecked in the stormy seas of the North Atlantic on a voyage to Buenos Aires in January 1882. Many of the ships built at Nefyn were comparatively large – ships such as the *Ann Alice* (97 tons) which was built in 1870, and the *Fanny Beck* (153 tons) which was built in 1864. The owner of this brigantine was Captain Hugh Roberts of Edern, who became one of the most successful shipowners on the river Tyne.

One of the main occupations in Nefyn was fishing in the bay and in the turbulent waters of Bardsey Sound. The *penwaig* [herring]of Nefyn were as famous as the *sgadan* [herring] of Aber-porth, and it is said that the fish caught on the northern side of Llŷn were quite a bit bigger than those caught in Aberdaron on the southern side of the peninsula. Although a number of the Nefyn fishermen followed their trade full-time, the herring shoals would also attract quarrymen, sailors and fishermen from Aberdaron, who would lodge in Nefyn between October and the end of January every year. Catching herring was an ancient pursuit in Nefyn, and it is said that there were as many as sixty-three boats operating from the town as early as 1287. By the early twentieth century, there were forty boats working out of Nefyn, each carrying a crew of three or four. These were local Llŷn rowing boats, some eighteen feet in length; unlike the Aberdaron or Bardsey boats, most of these craft had a prow at either end, and were always easy to launch at either high or low tide. One entrant in a National Eisteddfod competition in 1885 said:

> The quaint, old fishing and seafaring town is famous for the quantity of its herrings, this fish being found here in much better condition and of finer flavour than on the other side of the promontory of Llŷn. It is well known locally that the herrings taken along the northern coast of Llŷn are greatly esteemed and fetch a good price. Those on the other side in Cardigan Bay are not much more than half their size.

There were buildings for smoking and salting all along the shoreline at Nefyn, where the herring was prepared for shipping to Liverpool in particular.

It is difficult to imagine that there was enough confidence in the small village of Porth Dinllaen to make a bid to become the main port for a regular service to Ireland, but there was fierce competition over the matter between this little village and Holyhead. With the support of W.A. Maddocks (1773-1828), already renowned for his achievements at Porthmadog, the *Porthdinllaen Harbour Company* was formed in 1806. As well as improving the harbour, the company was also keen to attract more trade. Following the development of improved roads and railway links, and with Isambard Kingdom Brunel prepared, in 1845, to develop the *Worcester and Porthdinllaen Railway*, hopes were running high that the future of this remote port on the shores of Nefyn Bay would be secured. The plans were never realised, however, and consequently no Irish packet was ever seen at the quayside, and no passengers were ever able to enjoy the hospitality of the Tŷ Coch inn.

ii)   Caernarfon

The magnificent castle at Caernarfon was built in a location that was easy to defend, with the Menai Strait and the Afon Seiont creating an effective barrier to any attacks from the sea. With the castle dominating a large area of Snowdonia and Anglesey, the riverside wharfs were essential for the supply of its Anglo-Norman garrison. In time, a town developed beyond the castle walls, a town that relied on maritime trade. Slates from Dyffryn Nantlle – from the quarries of Dorothea, Cilgwyn, Pen-yr-orsedd and Hafod-las – were brought to Llechi Quay where they were loaded on ships bound for all parts of the world. It is said that more slates were exported from Caernarfon than from those ports that were specifically built for the slate trade at Y Felinheli and Porth Penrhyn (Bangor).

Of course the town of Caernarfon, on the shores of the Menai Strait, grew up some distance from the open sea. Although its waters are generally referred to as the *river* Menai in Welsh, according to the late Gwyn Pari Huws 'it is not strictly speaking a river but rather a gulf or straits connecting Caernarfon Bay at one end with Conwy Bay at the other. No, it is certainly not a river; it is part of the sea, its waters are salty and it is tidal along its whole length'. Negotiating the Menai Strait was not an easy task for sailing ships, as the fierce currents of the straits were extremely dangerous for ships and sailors alike. Nevertheless, despite all difficulties, trade and high quality shipbuilding were developed in the town of the 'Cofis' – the local name for the inhabitants of Caernarfon. It was a true sailor town, as it contained a large number of inns and houses of ill-repute, which were cheek by jowl with an equal proliferation of chapels of all denominations. Such was the demand for quay space in the town that it was felt that the old Llechi Quay, which had developed as a landing-place for the castle during the Middle Ages, was much too small. In 1868, therefore, the Caernarfon Harbour Trustees decided to build a new port, and in the early 1870s Victoria Dock was opened, and was considered by some optimists in the town to be the initial stage of a large-scale and very ambitious plan to build several docks along the banks of the Menai Strait. Unfortunately for them, following the development of the railways, the golden age of ports such as Caernarfon was coming to an end. In addition, after reaching its zenith in 1882, the Dyffryn Nantlle slate industry was also on the decline. The quarries were now linked to the railway and before very long the bustling trade of the little coastwise ships was undermined.

From the beginning of the nineteenth century up

until 1840, Caernarfon was considered to be subordinate to Beaumaris as a port, but from 1840 onwards Caernarfon became a port of registration for every ship from Y Felinheli to Barmouth, including Porthmadog and Pwllheli. As early as 1840, a fine building was erected for the Harbour Trust, at a time when the slate trade was actually receding somewhat. This remarkable building, which still acts as the main office for the port authority, stands on the Llechi Quay. Unlike the ports of Bangor and Y Felinheli, which belonged to aristocratic families such as the Douglas Pennant family, the port at Caernarfon was controlled by a public body, although the Assheton-Smith family of Y Faenol did have considerable influence on its operation. Slates were exported from Caernarfon to all parts of Britain and western Europe, and a considerable amount of trade developed with the United States, particularly with New York and Boston, and there was a big demand for ships, mainly schooners, to carry slates from Dyffryn Nantlle over the Atlantic. On the 16th of January 1858, the *Herald* newspaper reported:

> The demand for the best quality and best seconds is still in excess of supply . . . Large orders for the American market have been received during the week. In some instances, unable to get them executed at this port, the parties have gone to Port Madoc. We are gratified to learn that during the past year there has been a considerable increase in our slate export.

Ships were needed to deal with all the exports, and the shipbuilding industry, in the shadow of Caernarfon castle, became very important. It is said that over two hundred ships were built there between 1758 and 1898. To a great extent the industrial traders of Caernarfon had to depend on ships from other ports such as

Pwllheli and Porthmadog and, increasingly, on the shipbuilders of Canada, for ships to carry slate. With slate such a key commodity in the port's economy, there was not much space to develop shipyards for the construction of ships and sloops, and small brigs in particular were built on the banks of the Afon Seiont and in Victoria Dock. This dock was also the site of the 'Patent Slip', which was built to enable comparatively small ships to be drawn up for cleaning and repair.

Caernarfon was a leading slate port and all other activity was subordinate to the slate trade. However, a very important aspect of the port's activity was the provision of the means for emigration to America, and ships such as the barque the *Hindoo* sailed regularly to New York. An advertisement reads:

> The Fine Sailing Barque Hindoo of Caernarvon Burthen about 600 tons. The Sole Property of Mr H. Owen, Rhyddgar, Anglesey. Richard Hughes Commander will be ready to sail from this Port – about the 20th of March next with a ballast of slates. Emigrants will find the conveyance most convenient for embarking for the United States being properly fitted out for the accommodation of passengers.
>
> | Carnarvon | John Owen |
> |---|---|
> | 1st Febr. 1843 | High Street |

Very often, emigrants were considered to be a lot less valuable than slates, and the condition of some of the ships was atrocious. Although there were frequent direct passages from Caernarfon to the United States, Liverpool was the main port of embarkation for emigrants, and there was a popular regular service between Caernarfon and other ports in northern Wales and Liverpool. One of the most famous of the ships that took Welsh emigrants from Liverpool was the *Mimosa*, which in 1865 sailed to the other side of the world to establish Gwladfa Patagonia – the Welsh colony in Argentina. For many people, Liverpool was a port of farewell. There were a large number of emigration agents in Liverpool, many of whom were Welsh-speaking and were pillars of respectability in their chapels, and representatives in ports such as Caernarfon would arrange tickets and passage to distant countries.

Certainly during the nineteenth century Caernarfon was a true sea port. Most young lads in the town were attracted to a life at sea, and the whole atmosphere, smell and character of 'Cofis' Town' was bound up with the sea and its ships. There were all sorts of marine craftsmen, such as sail and ropemakers, and copper workers in foundries such as the famous de Winton Foundry. There were also insurance companies and, as one would expect in a port of this type, numerous schools of seamanship.

The most famous of these schools was the one under the auspices of Mrs Ellen Edwards (1820-1889). Mrs Edwards was a fervent Baptist who taught the complexities and mysteries of seamanship to generations of sailors. Her contribution was such that the Harbour Trust decided in 1888 to reward the contribution of a woman who, they said,

> really had conferred great benefit upon the seafaring population . . . by the marvellous success which had attended her teaching of young men.

In looking back on the tremendous activity that took place in Caernarfon up until about 1910, we should not perhaps forget the single-masted 60-ton flat, the *Ann*, which was built at Frodsham in 1799. This humble craft was immortalised in the verses of *Fflat Huw Puw*, which still feature in the Welsh folksong repertoire to this day. The *Ann* sailed until 1858, when she was wrecked on Tudwal Islands near Pwllheli. Although born in Liverpool in 1795, Captain Huw Puw spent his childhood in Caernarfon and became a true 'Cofi'.

iii)   Y Felinheli

The old village of Y Felinheli lies some three miles from Caernarfon on the banks of the Menai Strait. Its name derives from a flour mill that relied on the sea to drive its machinery. Nobody is quite sure of the location of this tidal mill, but there is no doubt that it was the development of the slate industry at the foot of Snowdon, some eight miles away, that provided the impetus for the development of Felinheli into a major harbour for the worldwide export of slates from the Dinorwig quarry. Y Felinheli had an enclosed dock built in 1824 which had a sluice gate, a dry dock for the repair of ships, stone wharves and plenty of room around the dock for the storage and preparation of slate for export. The dock was so important that for a while the name *Port Dinorwic* replaced the proper Welsh name. To link the huge quarry at Dinorwig with the port, a narrow-gauge railway was built in 1824 by a member of the Assheton-Smith family, who were the owners of the quarry, and this facilitated the journey to the top of the incline above the port. It was a horse-drawn railway, but by 1843 a decision was taken to lay a new track, which became known as the *Padarn Railway*; this railway had two steam locomotives, which drew laden wagons up from the Menai Strait.

During the second half of the nineteenth century in particular, there was tremendous activity on the quayside, and piles of high quality slates were in store, ready to be loaded onto one of the numerous ships moored there. Initially these were sailing vessels, but later steamships were also used.

It was at Y Felinheli, on the site of the present-day Dinas boat yard, that the largest wooden ship ever to be built in north Wales was completed in 1877: the 825-ton *Ordovic*. Some twenty-eight ships were built in Y Felinheli, most of them by Rees Jones of Barmouth, who had moved north in 1849 when activity had started to wane in that port. He was responsible for building twenty-eight schooners, three barques (including the *Ordovic*), and several barquentines and brigantines. Rees Jones and his son William owned important ships and held shares in the *Gwynedd Shipping Company*, which owned iron barques such as the *Moel Eilian*, the *Moel y Don* and the *Moel Tryvan* – all manufactured at William Doxford's yard in Sunderland. Aled Eames describes the *Moel Tryvan*, which sailed on its maiden voyage to the Far East under the command of Captain John Williams from Niwbwrch, with a crew from northern Wales:

> She took with her the financial hopes of many thrifty quarrymen from the Dinorwig area . . . of the first 143 shareholders 121 were quarrymen from the Llanberis, Deiniolen, Waunfawr and Rhostryfan area.

William E. Thomas of Y Felinheli was an influential owner of iron sailing ships in the last quarter of the nineteenth century. The company's offices remained in Y Felinheli, and much of its capital was raised locally from quarrymen, schoolteachers and Methodist ministers.

The port's main activity, however, was exporting the product of the huge Dinorwig quarry near Llanberis. This quarry covered some seven hundred acres, and at its height employed a workforce of some three thousand. In 1870, a number of iron and copper forges were built, in addition to engineering workshops of all types that met the requirements of such a large concern. The workshops at Gilfach Ddu were also responsible for all the work that had to be done on the railway engines and on the numerous steamships which, by the turn of the century, had almost entirely replaced the sailing ships.

Nowadays, there is very little to show for the immensity of the slate industry at Dinorwig. Today, the old port is full of ostentatious yachts, which are owned by foreign visitors who use their boats as gin palaces during the summer weekends, and who never venture out onto the Straits. Around the harbour there are a large number of tasteless flats that serve only the needs of the tourists. One of the most unacceptable twentieth century developments is the way in which the demand for second homes has replaced the traditional port communities. In Porth-cawl, Neyland, Porthmadog and here in Y Felinheli, the local planning authorities are greatly to blame for having allowed the once vibrant atmosphere and character of the communities to be destroyed.

iv)   Bangor and Porth Penrhyn

Of all the ports exporting slate in northern Wales, Porth Penrhyn near Bangor was among the busiest. Although Traeth Hirael had frequently been used as a landing-place prior to the nineteenth century, it was the completion of the narrow-gauge railway, some six and a half miles in length, from Bethesda to the sea, which brought real prosperity to the area. Previously, horse-drawn wagons had brought slates to the little harbour at Porth penrhyn. Each train of twenty-four wagons, piled high with slate, was pulled by two horses, and each team of horses was expected to complete six

journeys a day. The quarry at Bethesda was owned by
the Douglas-Pennant family: the Penrhyn Lords. Hard-
nosed and self-interested, they were loathed by the
quarrymen and community of Bethesda. In 1827, as a
display of the family's opulence, they built Penrhyn
Castle, an imperious mock-Norman castle that
reflected the authority and wealth of the family, whose
riches emanated from assets held both in Bethesda and
Jamaica. The castle stands on the peninsula between
the Afon Cegin to the west and the Afon Ogwen to the
east. It was here that Porth Penrhyn developed as a
new model harbour in 1790. With the advent of a steam
railway in the 1870s, Porth Penrhyn became extremely
prosperous, and as much as 100,000 tons of high
quality slate was reputedly exported annually, much of
it sent to north America. With his eye for business, Lord
Penrhyn was the owner of a substantial dock, but
during the final decade of the nineteenth century he
also owned a number of steamships, having bought up
the *Anglesey Shipping Company*, which owned the *S.S.
Pandora, Penrhyn, Harrier, Bangor, Lady Blanche* and
Pennant, as well as the *Mary B. Mitchell*, a three-masted
sailing ship. Slate exports declined considerably, and
although Porth Penrhyn is still occasionally used for
the export and import of goods, it is now
predominantly a mussel fishing port that exploits the
rich mussel beds of the Menai Strait. On the old
quayside, there are various small workshops, including
a shipwright's business. The occasional French ship
visits the harbour, mainly to collect cargoes of mussels,
which are popular fare in France.

Besides the activity on the quayside at Porth
Penrhyn, and long before the ambitious Lord Penrhyn
arrived on the scene, there was another established
centre of maritime activity on the other side of the bay,
around Hirael and Garth. A total of some sixty-four

ships were built here. The most famous of the Bangor shipbuilders was John Parry, who built some eleven ships, and Edward Ellis, who was responsible for nine ships. A modern boatyard, *Dickie's Boatyard*, is now the only reminder of the bustle that once existed in this part of Bangor. According to Aled Eames, who married Freda, the daughter of Dafydd W. Cale, the last sailmaker in Wales, in Hirael there was also:

> a foundry, a factory making writing-slates, chandlers, shops selling clothes and hardtack for the ships, and the workshops of skilled craftsmen such as shipwrights, blacksmiths and sailmakers. And among the little cottages on the seashore there were inns and lodging houses, chapels, the seamen's Institute, the Penlôn slate works, and on the lists of the Shipping Insurance Company at Plas Llwyd ('Y Clwb') there were over three hundred ships.

There was one important development in Bangor during the final decade of the nineteenth century, when there was a great deal of ill-feeling among the city's shopkeepers about the exorbitant charges that were imposed for bringing goods to the shops by rail. The charges at Porth Penrhyn were also fairly hefty and the traders were very reluctant to pay them. So, in 1891, the Garth quay was built (near the pier that was erected some five years later) where small steamers carrying goods to Bangor could discharge their cargo. The local name for the quay was the 'Ja Ja', and small steamers such as the *Christianna*, the *Medway*, the *St Seiriol* and the *St Tudwal* would run on a regular basis between Merseyside and northern Wales.

8.   ANGLESEY

i)   The ports of Anglesey

The fact that Anglesey is surrounded by the sea and, until the building of Telford's bridge at the beginning of the nineteenth century, lacked a dry link with the mainland, ensured that the maritime tradition was vital to the island. The link between its coastal villages and the rest of the world was essential to the inhabitants. Their livelihood depended on maritime trade: agricultural produce and industrial materials were exported from a host of tiny villages. Penmon, for example, exported millstone grit, while at Traeth Coch Bay, a limestone that resembled marble was shipped out. This commodity proved extremely popular, and reputedly some two hundred individuals were employed at Traeth Coch quarry. Up until around 1860, coal was mined in the centre of the island, particularly in the Malltraeth and Pentre Berw area, but very little was exported. In the sixteenth century, there is a reference to a cargo of coal being exported from Beaumaris to Ayr, and another to France.

There was also a certain amount of shipbuilding in the coastal villages of Anglesey, and there is no doubt that the sea attracted a large number of its men. It is said, for example, that Newborough was the breeding ground for as many sailors as any maritime village in Wales, and for many centuries Beaumaris was the main shipping registry for northern Wales. The town of Beaumaris, whose port dates back to the era of the castles, controlled all sea traffic from Barmouth in the south to Chester in the north. In 1797 over seven hundred ships were on the Beaumaris register, although very few of these would actually visit the port there. According to Lewis Morris, 'Beaumaris was a place of good trade formerly and might be still if the inhabitants pursued it, it being an excellent harbour, well situated and well supplied with the gifts of nature'.

Despite the fact that a large number of villages in Anglesey enjoyed maritime activity – from Moelfre to Cemaes Bay on the eastern side, and from Aberffraw to Llanfaethlu on the west – these were very much subordinate to Menai Bridge, Holyhead and Amlwch, the big ports on the island.

ii)   Menai Bridge

Before the bridges were built over the Menai Strait during the nineteenth century, crossing the straits between Anglesey and Arfon was very difficult because of its fierce currents. In the absence of a bridge, there were regular ferries running from one side to the other, carrying all manner of cargo: passengers, livestock (cattle, pigs and sheep) and a variety of commodities. For passengers from Dublin, the Menai Strait was the most dangerous part of their journey between Holyhead and London, although a main road had reached the shores of the Menai Strait by the latter half of the eighteenth century. The main ferries that crossed the straits were the Abermenai ferry; the Tan-y-foel ferry to Caernarfon; the Moel-y-don ferry to Y Felinheli; the Menai Bridge ferry; the Porth-yr-Esgob ferry; the Garth ferry to Bangor; the Beaumaris ferry, and the Llan-faes ferry. With the construction of Telford's bridge in 1826 and Britannia Bridge in 1850, communication between Anglesey and the mainland became much easier. One village to take advantage of this was Menai Bridge (Y Borth). In the days before the bridge was built, the crossing from Bangor to Menai

Bridge was very important, and horses and carriages and their passengers would have to venture across the Menai Strait in rowing boats, which were less than robust. It was now possible to travel safely and unimpeded over the bridge.

Although compared to the bustle of Bangor and Caernarfon there was little maritime activity in Menai Bridge itself until about 1840, there was a certain amount of shipbuilding and importing of timber and other essentials. Then, around 1843, the Davies family rose to eminence as prominent shipowners. Between 1843 and 1905 this family owned some eighty sailing ships worldwide, many of which were crewed by men from Anglesey and Arfon. The transport of guano from Peru and Chile was clearly the most profitable trade for the Davies family, such that this wealthy nautical dynasty became known to the people of Menai Bridge as *Teulu Baw Adar* (the birdshit family). Aled Eames describes them as being a particularly narrow-minded brand of Calvinistic Methodist, and comments:

> it is odd to think that many of the chapels and elementary schools of northern Wales were built from money earned from *guano*, but it should also be remembered that their venture provided work – very hard work – on their ships for hundreds of young men from the area. When Richard Davies was elected Member of Parliament, the first non-conformist to represent Anglesey, a photograph was taken to celebrate the occasion, showing over fifty officers who were serving on their ships . . . we would be able to trace the career of almost every one of them; the overwhelming majority of them originated from Gwynedd, but some also came from Pembrokeshire and Ceredigion.

The Davies family came from Llangefni, and Richard Davies, who was born in 1778, ran a prosperous business there which sold everything. He imported goods from Liverpool to the Llanbedr-goch and Traeth Coch area on the eastern seaboard of Anglesey, and sold goods to the local quarrymen at low prices. In 1828 the family set up a timber yard not far from the site of Telford's new bridge, and imported timber from the Baltic countries and, subsequently, from Canada. Richard Davies' eldest son, John, was responsible for the development of Menai Bridge, while the second son, Robert, worked in a foundry at Caernarfon, and Richard himself was in charge of the business at Traeth Coch and was responsible for the export of stone to Liverpool. Before long, the family realised that the future lay in Menai Bridge, and that future was based on ships sailing to north America, rather than from Amlwch or Bangor. Despite their hardline Methodism, the Davies' ships from Menai Bridge were involved in the slave trade. They also carried emigrants to the New World. With large vessels such as the *Enterprise*, the *Agnes* and the *Courtney*, all built by shipbuilders in Canada and New England, incredible wealth poured into Menai Bridge. Unlike many other shipping companies, the company headquarters remained in Menai Bridge right up to its closure in 1905. As staunch and teetotal Methodists, the contribution of members of the Davies family to the religious life of northern Wales was immense: they funded chapels and schools and even the Cartref Bontnewydd children's home to the south of Caernarfon, which still operates to this day.

iii)   Holyhead

Holyhead is different from all other ports in northern Wales, in that it was not built in response to local demand and, over the centuries, its development has not been dependent on the import and export of goods. The interaction between Ireland and Britain is responsible for the existence of both the town and the port, and as this part of Anglesey is closest to Dublin, Ireland has exerted a strong influence for many centuries. Today, Holyhead is the main port in Britain handling trade between Ireland and Britain, and the daily ferry service provided by *Irish Ferries* and *Stena* who carry passengers and goods, are of vital importance.

In addition to being a port specially designed to provide a regular service to Ireland, the sheltered bay at Holyhead was considered to be a refuge for sailing ships. Many ships could be found there at any one time, in particular during stormy weather. For example Susan Campbell Jones observes: 'As late as 1917, over a period of eleven weeks, more than 250 vessels were windbound there.'

It was here too that ships from Liverpool would anchor, while they waited for the right wind to send them off on their distant voyages.

However, it was during the time of the turbulent connection between England and her fiercely independent colony in Ireland that Holyhead became established from as early as 1570 as the main port for the transport of troops and all kinds of passengers. One of the main problems that faced the British government over the centuries was how to find the most effective way of ruling Ireland. The successful government of an insurgent colony depended to a great extent on efficient communications. In the south, ports such as

Neyland and Fishguard were developed as service centres, while in the north several lesser ports such as Aberdyfi and Porth Dinllaen expressed their ambition to become ferry ports. However, in spite of everything, it was the harbour on the western coast of Anglesey that was successful. During the sixteenth century, when a shipping service was first established there, Holyhead was a fairly remote location. It was a long way from the centre of government and power in London, and the road across England and the mountains of northern Wales was difficult and dangerous. As if that were not enough, the Menai Strait also had to be crossed before Anglesey could be reached. Nevertheless, despite all the difficulties, Holyhead became the main port for passengers and goods and, in particular, the Royal Mail.

Holyhead was a rather dismal place as it was described by the poet Jonathan Swift:

> Lo, here I sit at Holyhead
> With muddy ale and mouldy bread,
> I'm fastened bole with wind and tide
> I see the ships at anchor side,
> The Captain swears, the sea's too rough
> (He has not passengers enough)
> And thus the Dean is forced to stay
> Till others come to help the pay.

Lewis Morris, one of the most famous sons of Anglesey, who worked at Holyhead, had an opportunity to promote the port and to support its trade. He makes reference to three effective services which were offered between Holyhead and Ireland, and he was very keen to see improvements at the port 'for the Irish to import their goods that pay English duty'. Morris gives the following account of the exports from the port in 1747:

There was shipped off here of different kind of grain – twenty two thousand bushells – in addition to supplies like butter, cheese and bacon . . . Much profit was made from burning a plant growing on the sea rocks called by the natives *Gwymon* – into a kind of salt called kelp. One of the ingredients in making glass and used also in Allum works.

Notwithstanding Morris' recommendations, the export trade from Holyhead was minimal, and it was the passenger and postal service which predominated. Following the Act of Union between England and Ireland, great improvements were made in the harbour. A little later, in 1815, Thomas Telford developed the new main road overland from London, which crossed the Menai Strait by means of his splendid bridge. With transport along the roads somewhat better than had been the case before, the Royal Mail service was established in 1820 with fast ferries, which created an effective link between London and Dublin. Unfortunately, although this service was successful, the opening of the railway to Merseyside and Liverpool, which offered a better service than the Royal Mail stagecoach to Anglesey, meant that the port faced more trouble. In 1838, the post went by rail to Liverpool and from there to Dublin. After a long, hard battle, better times arrived when the *Chester and Holyhead Railway* was completed in 1850. The company built four new paddle ships and started a regular service to Ireland, but another Ireland-based company entered the fray from 1843 onwards, and enjoyed a considerable degree of success. This was the *City of Dublin Steam Packet Company*. After its merger with *The Liverpool & Llandudno and Welsh Coast Steamboat Co. Ltd* in 1881, this became the most important of the shipping companies involved in services to and from Holyhead. In 1891 it merged with the *New North Wales Steamship Co. Ltd* to form the *Liverpool and North Wales Steamship Co. Ltd*. This company won the contract to carry the Royal Mail from then on up until the 1920s. In the same way as in Pembrokeshire, it seemed that it was the railway companies at Holyhead that were to be responsible for both the ships and the ports. Thus, in 1920, the *London and North Western Railway* built four new ships for the service between Holyhead and Dun Laoghaire. In 1923, it was the *London Midland and Scottish Railway* that took on the mantle.

Of course, since 1945, there have been tremendous changes in the ferry services to Ireland. As the transport of lorries and cars is now the main role played by these ships, there have been sweeping changes in their design and size. Ships to carry passengers from one port to another are no longer what is required and, as a result, the port at Holyhead has had to be modified to accommodate the embarkation and disembarkation of huge vehicles. In 1965 there were further improvements, and since that time more and more has been done to deal with larger and larger vessels. When *Sealink* was swallowed up by the huge *Stena* concern, the connection with the railways was broken, and with *Irish Ferries* building larger ships, the port of Holyhead at the beginning of the twenty-first century is doing well.

iv)   Amlwch

The port of Amlwch is unique in Wales, not only because it was built towards the end of the eighteenth century for the sole purpose of exporting the product of Europe's main copper workings, but also because this is the only port in Wales which faces north. Since it was built, the port has taken a considerable battering from the north winds, and on occasion big storms have inflicted substantial damage in and around its narrow dock.

Until the second half of the eighteenth century, the harbour at Amlwch was a small and rather insignificant affair and, according to Lewis Morris:

> It provided no more than an insecure refuge for small ships, no more than a cove between two steep rocks where a vessel hath no room to wind, even at high water.

After the discovery of huge deposits of copper at Parys Mountain near the north coast of Anglesey in 1768, the ensuing changes had a truly spectacular impact on the area. With a sparse population and without any convenient means of exporting the copper from this remote spot, there were serious problems to be addressed. In 1793, an Act was passed to extend, deepen and clean out the port of Amlwch. Thousands thronged to the area in search of work, and as many as fifteen hundred miners, men and women alike (the latter known as 'Copar Ladis'), are said to have worked on Parys Mountain, in the most dangerous and unhealthy conditions.

One of the founders of the Parys Mountain and Porth Amlwch copper industry was a man called Thomas Williams, a local lawyer and businessman who became renowned throughout the country as *Twm Chwarae Teg* [fair play]. It was he who built the enormous smelter on the banks of the Dee near Treffynnon. He was also astute enough to realise that there was a tremendous demand for copper sheets to sheath the bottom of the ships of the Royal Navy, particularly in times of war. Not only did the copper protect the vessels from the *teredo* worms that attacked the ship's timbers, but copper-bottomed ships were also said to be faster and easier to steer, and saved heavy and frequent costs. Thomas Williams, the Copper King, was a very wealthy and successful entrepreneur, and although he was known as *Twm Chwarae Teg*, in fact he was an extremely exploitative man, and was considered to be very harsh by his fellow industrialists.

As in almost every town that experienced rapid growth, rather like the Wild West in America, Amlwch and its port were somewhat unsavoury places. There were over sixty pubs and other dubious establishments in the town, and gangs of workers fought under the yellow smog that belched from the thirty-one copper smelters which operated locally. It is no wonder that the churches of Amlwch found it difficult to attract any ministers or priests to look after the religious institutions in the town.

To meet the needs of Amlwch's miners and sailors, there were plenty of craftsmen available in the rest of the island. From the mid-nineteenth century, for example, nearby Llannerch-y-medd was home to some two hundred and fifty cobblers, who were kept busy making boots and shoes for the workers and miners of Parys Mountain. In Amlwch itself there was a large brewery – Greenhalls of St Helens – which was established in the town at almost the same time as the renewal of the harbour in 1786. Another famous product was Amlwch tobacco. The town's tobacco works produced shag of different strengths and types suitable for chewing or smoking, as well as a variety of snuffs, and in his report to the Royal Commission on employment in 1855 D. Lleufer Thomas observes: 'Practically everyone smokes or chews or does both. By the end of each meeting I held, the floor was covered with tobacco spittle.'

Amlwch in the nineteenth century was obviously a rough and unruly sort of place, but by the end of that century, following the discovery of copper in other parts of the world, the industry here went into decline. However, the wasteland of Parys Mountain, devoid of all grass and trees, still dominates the landscape around the now idle port and town.

When the port was in its heyday, shipbuilding developed at Amlwch, and two yards operated here – Paynter's yard, or *Iard Ochr Draw* [the yard on the other side] on the left-hand side of the harbour, and *Yr Iard Newydd* [the new yard] or William Thomas' yard, to the south-east of the harbour. A yard was also set up by the Treweek family from Cornwall, one of whose number, James Treweek, was employed as an agent at the Parys Mountain works. In 1872 the Treweek shipyard was bought by a local businessman, Captain William Thomas, a shipowner, master and chandler. Aled Eames observes:

> By 1872 Captain Thomas had a thriving ship chandler's business, a large store house for all kinds of building materials brought into Amlwch by his own coastal smacks, and he had a busy shipyard where the noise of the caulker's mallets, the saws and the adzes, the smell of the stack of timber and the general air of brisk industry was to continue for over thirty years.

Although William Thomas built a number of wooden schooners in the 1870s and 1880s, he was best known for his iron ships. His schooners, such as the *Elizabeth Peers*, the *Cymric* and the *Gaelic*, among a large number of similar vessels, were considered to be particularly graceful, and several of them he designed and built for a shipowner from Denmark, such as the *Detlev Wagner*, which he built in 1891. Shipowners from the Millom

276

and Duddon area were good customers of the Amlwch yard, and iron and steel was imported to the yard from Cumbria. A second shipyard was established by William Thomas, and a large number of Amlwch workers went to Millom and set up a Welsh chapel and society in that town. The last ship of the Thomas family of Amlwch was the schooner *Eilean* in 1908, a ship which was still around during the final decade of the twentieth century.

9. FROM CONWY TO DEESIDE

i) Conwy

To the east of Bangor, the coast is rather open and unsheltered and has no substantial estuaries before the Afon Conwy. The terrain is not suitable for building a port. Goods were in fact unloaded on the beaches of Abergwyngregyn (or Aber) and a pier for loading granite for export all over Europe is still to be seen at Llanfairfechan and Penmaenmawr. There also used to be a fair amount of activity on Traeth Lafan, the name given to the sands which lie between Anglesey and Arfon. The main shipping lanes for the Menai Strait lie on the eastern side of the bay, which is why it was Beaumaris that developed as the major port in the area.

Although stone, slate and timber were landed on the open beach at Llandudno for the building of its houses and grand hotels when it was developing into the main holiday resort of northern Wales, the only port of any significance was Conwy. An early port developed, initially to meet the needs of the invading armies, near Edward I's splendid castle at the mouth of the estuary of the Conwy. In time, this port became more significant in the history of Welsh seamanship. With Thomas Telford's graceful bridge, which was built in 1826, and with its spectacular estuary, Conwy has a great deal to offer. It has also contributed significantly to the shipbuilding industry: between 1758 and 1891 a total of one hundred and twenty-eight large ships were built in different spots near the town walls, by shipbuilders such as Thomas Roberts, John Roberts, Richard Thomas and John Jones and their craftsmen. The largest vessel to be built here was the 304-ton brig the *Palanquin*, which launched in 1842 by John Jones. Between 1819 and 1853 the main vessels produced by the yards were schooners of up to some 80 tons, most of which were sailed by mariners from Conwy itself. Some ships were built several miles up-river around Caerhun, and for several years Robert Roberts of Caerhun was responsible for building some very notable schooners.

There was a fair amount of traffic between the port of Conwy and the outside world, and although not a great deal was exported from the town other than cargoes of ore, copper and slate, there were occasional imports of timber, particularly for the construction of ships and fishing boats. The quay was erected between the town walls and the river in 1835, and it was there that big ships from the Baltic and Scandinavia would regularly discharge their cargoes. Today, with its hundreds of leisure craft, it is easy to think of Conwy as little more than a playground for the rich, but the harbour does have another side. Although cargo ships no longer come to the quay, the fishing industry is still fairly important here. Despite many problems, the old skill of gathering mussels continues at the mouth of the river. A historian in 1835 states:

> The *cragen las* is found in abundance on the bar at the mouth of the river and great quantities of the mussels are daily gathered by a number of industrious people.

Until about the mid-nineteenth century there was pearl fishing in the estuary as well as further upstream near Trefriw but, due to over-exploitation and the influx of fishermen to Conwy from all over the country, the source was soon exhausted. The gathering of mussels for markets in northern England persisted somewhat longer. According to tradition, only four families had the right to gather mussels in the Conwy. Members of these families, both men and women, would venture out into the estuary from the quay in 18 to 30 foot rowing boats, each equipped with a long rake with which to scrape the bottom of the river. It was the women's task to gather mussels from rocks on the shoreline. The four families in question were Jones, Roberts, Hughes and Craven, and woe betide any one who attempted to transgress the strict rules governing the river.

ii)   Y Rhyl and Deeside

From the Great Orme to the old coal mine, Point of Ayr, north-eastern Wales seems to be nothing more than a land of caravan sites, second homes and summertime entertainments. The sea goes out a long way at low tide and leaves open sandy beaches that attract city dwellers in their droves. Apart from the lime quarry and a wharf built for the export of lime at Llanddulas, until recently the towns and villages along this coast were primarily the creation of the tourist industry. Places such as Rhos-on-Sea, Abergele, Prestatyn, Colwyn Bay and Gronant are full of attractions to entertain the crowds. Although Rhyl is probably the most tasteless of these seaside settlements, one part of the town does in fact have a maritime tradition. Around Voryd, where the Clwyd flows into the sea, a port developed – a port that was devoted mainly to the import of timber for the large timber yard belonging to Charles Jones and Sons. With all the building work taking place in the seaside towns and villages in this region, there was a great demand for timber and building materials, and for some years Voryd was extremely busy. Today, despite the hazards of the Clwyd estuary, it is from here that local fishermen operate. Most of their catch is sold locally.

The area to the east of the village of Talacre and the old coastal pit of Point of Ayr is quite different in character. This is the old industrial area of Deeside, with its working towns and villages such as Ffynnongroyw, Mostyn, Connah's Quay, Flint, Bagillt, Llannerch-y-môr and Shotton – which at one time were home to a range of industries and centres of importance to sailors. 'Llongau Afon Gaer' [the river Chester ships] was the name given to vessels that navigated the narrow channels of the Dee. In Roman times, it was possible to sail as far upstream as Chester itself, but over time there have been enormous changes in the river's course, and shifting sand banks have resulted in the closure of one harbour after another along the estuary. All efforts to clear the channel to Chester were in vain: at Queensferry, for example, canals were dug in an attempt to overcome the problem, but to no avail. During the eighteenth century, the regular service to Ireland was moved from Chester to Parkgate, but very quickly the sand filled up that old harbour too. Today, the dock wall is about a mile from the river, behind the sandy marsh of Dawnpool Bank, which is home to diverse birdlife. At one time, the village of Hoylake used to be one of the main fishing villages on the Dee, but the connection with the river was broken very soon. One by one, the maritime trade of the communities along the river was destroyed. This was almost entirely due to the impact of the shifting sandbanks. Nowadays, it is only Mostyn that remains as some sort of working port. There was great investment in Mostyn during the first two years of the present century and the docks were extended in order to accommodate the new service offered by P&O to Dublin. Despite the difficulties of navigating the Dee, an optimistic observer notes in the magazine *Sea Breezes:*

To see Mostyn in 2003 is a lesson on how old ports can be revitalised. The small dock may have been mentally written off by economic agencies on a number of occasions as a relic from its days serving outdated iron works and worn out collieries. It could so easily have been tarted up as a marine basin with European cash, to fill with plastic boats that don't go anywhere and surrounded by apartments for Scousers and Mancunians thinking themselves into a kind of North Wales San Tropez. But fortunately that didn't happen and many people are earning a 21st century living geared to high tech engineering from the revitalised port.

With the huge developments at the nearby Airbus factory at Brychtyn and the construction of off-shore wind farms, Mostyn is once again becoming an important place. That, at least, is the hope and the dream, but of course there are objections to the proposals by conservation groups.

In March 2004, Mostyn received bad news, when P&O decided to end its daily goods service to Dublin, despite the millions that had been spent on improving the resources at Mostyn Docks. After a promising start in November 2001, two large ships were acquired to maintain the service. The 24,206-ton *European Ambassador*, which was built in Japan in 2001, and the 18,653-ton *European Envoy*, which is also from Japan, ran regularly for just over a year. The decline in trade was blamed on the condition of the Dee estuary, with its shifting sandbanks and unstable channel. The P&O ships often hit sandbanks and the authorities were blamed for being unwilling to spend money on dredging.

At one time, a number of other villages along the shores of the river were also busy. All of these are now rather dismal places. The British Rail ferry the *Duke of Lancaster* is perhaps the best symbol of the decline: this ship, which dates back to the 1950s, has been stuck on the sands for thirty years at Llannerch-y-môr. It is gradually rusting away, and all attempts to turn it into a leisure and retail centre have failed.

In the 1830s and 1840s, the river was quite active. Flint was a busy port that exported coal and imported timber, but within a few years the course of the river had changed, and ships bypassed Flint for Mostyn and Connah's Quay. Aled Eames argues that:

> By the 1860s Connah's Quay was the main port in the area. The *Wrexham, Mold and Connah's Quay Railway* built a railway and docks and although the population of the town was not large, the shipyards, chandlers and sail lofts were all kept busy. The seafaring families of this community became well known to sailors all over Britain – Coppack, Vickers, Bennett, Reney, Hughes, Bithel, Foulkes and others.

The ships of Connah's Quay sailed the length of the coast of Britain and to Europe carrying a variety of goods, from Buckley pottery to Ruabon bricks, and they imported timber from Scandinavia and iron from Spain. There was great activity, and Connah's Quay attracted seamen from all over northern Wales.

The shipbuilding industry, particularly the building of large sailing ships, was a major activity on the Dee. In 1855, for example, the famous *Royal Charter* was built there by William Patterson of Sandycroft. This was an iron ship of 2,719 tons, which was driven by sails and a steam engine. While returning from Australia on the 26th of October 1859, the ship was wrecked on the rocks at Moelfre, with a loss of 434 lives and an extremely valuable cargo.

The three-masted schooner, the *Kathleen and May*,

was built under the name *Lizzie May* for the Coppack Brothers, and was still sailing in 2004. This schooner was built by the main shipbuilders on the river, Ferguson and Baird – Scots who had established themselves in Flint and Connah's Quay in around 1858. The ships which they built – over fifty of them – were considered to be of the highest quality, and included ships such as the *Charles Edwards*, the *Earl Cairns*, the *Agnes Craig*, the *Windermere* and the *Lizzie May*. There were several other companies such as *Ashburner, Barrow & Co.* who had some ten ships to their name, and *Reney* who had a dozen or more schooners.

The most famous shipping company on the shores of the Dee was the Coppack brothers' company from Connah's Quay. The Kopecks or Kopocks originated from Norway and came to the Dee with a cargo of lime during the seventeenth century. Unfortunately, the ship filled with water and the lime solidified completely, and there was no hope of unloading it. After that the family sailed for a while as crew members on Deeside ships. In October 1860, however, Captain John Coppack decided to leave the sea, and he established a shipping company in the front room of his house in Connah's Quay. There was a big demand for a service to export Halkyn lead, Shotton steel, coal from Point of Ayr and bricks from Ruabon and Buckley to all over Europe. There was a demand for the import of iron ore and many other raw materials for the important industrial area of Deeside.

With a number of locally-built schooners, the Coppack business flourished, and in 1881 they acquired their first steamship, the *Aston*, bought especially for the export of bricks from Buckley to Ireland.

The company continued to sail the coasts until 1971, when the last of their steamers – the *Vauban* and the

Indurita – were sold by members of the same family who had originally established the company over a century earlier.

Selected Bibliography

Balchin, W.G.V. (ed.), *Swansea and its region* (1971).

Bennet, P. a David Jenkins, *Welsh Ports of the Great Western Railway* (1994).

Campbell-Jones, Susan (Gweler hefyd S. Passmore), *Welsh Sail* (1976).

Cymru a'r Môr/Maritime Heritage, Cylchgrawn Blynyddol ers 1976.

Coppack, T., *A Lifetime with Ships* (Afon Dyfrdwy) (1973).

Daunton, Martin, *Coal Metropolis*, Cardiff 1870-1914 (1977).

Davies, Donald, *Those were the Days*, 2 gyfrol, Aberteifi (1991).

Davies, John, *Cardiff and the Marquesses of Bute* (1981).

Davies, Margaret, *The Story of Tenby* (1979).

Eames, Aled,
- *O Bwllheli i Bendraw'r Byd* (1979).
- *Heb Long wrth y Cei* (1989).
- *Y Fordaith Bell* (1993).
- *Machlud Hwyliau Cymru* (1984).
- *Ships and Seamen of Anglesey* (1973).
- *Porthmadog Ships* (1975).
- *Ventures in Sail* (1987).

Edwards, John (Golygydd), *Tinopolis*, Llanelli (1995).

Elis-Williams, M., *Packet to Ireland* (1984).

Evans, Catherine, Steve Dodsworth and Julie Bennett, *Below the Bridge, A Photo Historical Survey of Cardiff Dockland to 1983* (1984).

Fishlock, Trevor, *Fishlock's Sea Stories* (2003).

Hughes, Henry,
- *Immortal Sails*
- *Through Mighty Seas*, Porthmadog (1975).

Jeffreys, D.E., *Maritime Memories of Cardiff* (1978).

Jenkins, David,
- *Shipping at Cardiff – Photographs from the Hanson Collection* (1993).
- *Shipowners of Cardiff* (1997).

Jenkins, J. Geraint,
- *The In-Shore Fishermen of Wales* (1991).
- *Llangrannog* 1998: 2002: 2004.
- *Maritime Heritage – The Ships and Seamen of Southern Ceredigion* (1982).

Jenkins, J. Geraint and David Jenkins,
- *Cardiff Shipowners* (1986).
- *The Maritime Heritage of Dyfed* (1982).

John, Brian, *Ports and Harbours of Pembrokeshire* (1976).
Jones, J.M.O., *Morwyr y Cilie* (2002).
Lewis, L. Haydn, *Penodau yn Hanes Aberaeron a'r Cylch* (1970).
Lewis, W.J.,
   – *Born on a Perilous Rock.* – *Aberystwyth, Past and Present* (1980).
   – *The Gateway to Wales* – *A History of Cardigan* (1990).
Lloyd, Lewis,
   – *The Port of Caernarfon 1793-1900* (1989).
   – *Maritime Merioneth* – *The Town and Port of Barmouth* (1971).
   – *The Unity of Barmouth* (1977).
   – *Sails on the Mawddach* (1981).
   – *The Amity of Aberdyfi* (1983).
Lewis, M.J.T., *Sails on the Dwyryd* (1989).
Lloyd-Hughes, D.G., *Pwllheli* (1991).
Lodwick J. & V., *The Story of Carmarthen* (1994).
Moore, Donald (Gol.), *Barry* – *The Centenary Book* (1986).
Morgan, D., *The Cardiff Story* (1991).
Morgan, Alun, *Porthcawl, Newton and Nottage* (1987).
Morgan, D.W., *Brief Glory*, Aberdyfi (1948).
Nicholson, J.A., *Pembrey and Burry Port* (1993).
O'Neill, Dan, *Tiger Bay and the Docks* (2001).
Pari-Huws, Gwyn, *Y Fenai* (2002).
Passmore, S.G., *Farmers and Figureheads, The Port of New Quay and its Hinterland* (1992).
Parker, Mike, *Coast to Coast* (2003).
Paggett, Paul, *Solva* (1990).
Rees, J.F., *The Milford Story* (1954).
Takel, R., *The Story of Ports and Shipping along the Glamorgan Heritage Coast* (1982).
Thomas, David,
   – *Hen Longau Sir Gaernarfon* (1952).
   – *Hen Longau a Llongwyr Cymru* (1949).
Troughton, William, *Aberystwyth Harbour* (1997).
Williams, Glanmor (Gol.), *Swansea* (1990).

Index

Sefydliad Astudiaethau Hanes Morwrol Cymru

MOROL

Institute of Welsh Maritime Historical Studies

MOROL (Sefydliad Astudiaethau Hanes Morwrol Cymru – Institute of Welsh Maritime Historical Studies) was established in 2005 with the aim of promoting interest and research in the maritime history of Wales and in furthering international links. MOROL's inaugural event was the Aled Eames Memorial Lecture given by Dr David Jenkins of the National Waterfront Museum on the subject *Toilers of the Sea*. The lecture was an acknowledgment of the contribution of the late Aled Eames to Welsh, and international, maritime history delivered by one of Wales' leading contemporary maritime historians.

Similarly it is with one eye on the past and one to the future that MOROL, in conjunction with Gwasg Carreg Gwalch, presents this new series on Welsh maritime history. The aim is to publish new work by established maritime historians alongside a selection of well-known publications no longer in print. The series will publish in both Welsh and English (including translations of key Welsh texts) on a variety of maritime topics. It is appropriate that the first two publications in this series provide, on the one hand, a general national history of Welsh maritime communities in Geraint Jenkins' *Welsh Ships and Sailing Men* while, on the other, David Thomas' *Hen Longau Sir Gaernarfon*, is a detailed regional study whose re-publication is long overdue.

MOROL wishes to acknowledge Myrddin ap Dafydd and Gwasg Carreg Gwalch's invaluable support in ensuring the success of this series.